HIGH PRAISE FOR
MAX DAVIS AND

Never Stick Your Tongue Out at Mama

"COMPELLING . . . THIS BOOK IS BOTH A
FUN-READ AND A MUST-READ . . . Max
Davis uses a breezy style to share his life-changing
message."
  —Criswell Freeman, author of *When Life Throws
      You a Curveball, Hit It*

"A DELIGHTFUL BOOK . . . it overflows with
insight on reaching your full potential."
  —Morris Alexander, Ph.D., clinical psychologist

"MUST READING FOR THOSE INTER-
ESTED IN OPTIMAL HEALTH AND WELL-
BEING . . . Max communicates the truth about
mental health and spiritual renewal with love and
laughter."
  —Terry Dorian, author of *Health Begins in Him*

"Insightful essays dealing with life's trials and trea-
sures . . . Emotional, but with a head on its shoulders."
            —Gerald Laurence, *On the Scene*

QUANTITY SALES

Most Dell books are available at special quantity discounts when purchased in bulk by corporations, organizations, or groups. Special imprints, messages, and excerpts can be produced to meet your needs. For more information, write to: Dell Publishing, 1540 Broadway, New York, NY 10036. Attention: Director, Special Markets.

INDIVIDUAL SALES

Are there any Dell books you want but cannot find in your local stores? If so, you can order them directly from us. You can get any Dell book currently in print. For a complete up-to-date listing of our books and information on how to order, write to: Dell Readers Service, Box DR, 1540 Broadway, New York, NY 10036.

Never Stick Your Tongue Out at Mama

And Other Life-Transforming Revelations

Max Davis

A DELL TRADE PAPERBACK

A DELL TRADE PAPERBACK
Published by
Dell Publishing
a division of
Bantam Doubleday Dell Publishing Group, Inc.
1540 Broadway
New York, New York 10036

Permissions appear on pages 165–166.

ISBN: 0-440-50802-9

Reprinted by arrangement with Delacorte Press

Printed in the United States of America

Published simultaneously in Canada

December 1998

10 9 8 7 6 5 4 3 2 1

BVG

To my dearest Alanna,

The Rocky Mountains pale

beside your beauty,

both inner and outer.

Acknowledgments

A project such as this has no hope of completion without the assistance of many selfless people. First I would like to thank my wife, Alanna, for all her encouragement, patience, and wisdom. Her intelligent input was the balance this book needed. I am most grateful to my editor, Mary Ellen O'Neill, and to my agent, Meredith Bernstein, for all their hard work and encouragement. Also, I want to give a special thanks to Don Pippen of Best Books, Inc., Criswell Freeman of Walnut Grove Press, and Maryglenn McCombs of Dowling Press. You guys are more than business associates. You are true friends. Your advice has been pure gold to my career. Thanks to all the investors in Enhance Publishing for believing in this vision. Thank you to Gerald and Sharon Phares for believing in me, listening to my ideas, and giving me that extra encouragement I needed to get over the hump. Finally, thanks, Mom and Dad, for loving me through all the ups and downs.

Contents

1. Never Stick Your Tongue Out at Mama   1

2. Even Toddlers Do It   13

3. Monsters Under the Bed   23

4. Barking at the Coach's Wife   36

5. Risky Business   43

6. What an Incredible Thought!   54

7. Difficult People   58

8. Computers and Tractors   72

9. Appreciation for Appreciation   82

10. Total Freedom   90

11. KA-BOOM!   107

12. $1 Makes a Big Difference   118

13. Four Damaged Vehicles   131

14. Failing Forward   147

15. A Serious Subject   159

Never
Stick
Your
Tongue
Out at
Mama

1

Never Stick
Your Tongue
Out at Mama

DID YOU EVER get a whipping? I don't
mean a couple of slaps on the hand or a few
whacks on the derriere, either. I mean an old-
fashioned, Jim Dandy whippin'. You do know
there's a big difference, don't you? I can't remember how many spankings I got growing up,
but I can tell you exactly how many whippin's I
got! Three—*uno, dos, tres*. I know. I know. I'm
perfectly aware that an intense debate rages
over the long-term effects of physical punishment. Talking positively about it is not popular
these days. I'm also aware that some people
reading this book, perhaps many, were victims
of unhealthy physical punishment. Please un-

derstand, I would never excuse abuse in any form or fashion. You'll get no argument from me that physical punishment, if used, should be few and far between, and under controlled conditions.

For the record, my mom and dad were the most loving, caring parents anyone could hope for. Oh, they made their share of mistakes, as all parents do. But parenting is no picnic. It's a tough assignment! I should know; I have three children of my own. Parenting involves a whole lot of "should I's" and "what ifs" and "I just don't knows." I've skimmed through a plethora of books on parenting. Some offer helpful insight. Yet good parenting, in my opinion, boils down to two basic elements: loving your children unconditionally and doing the best you can. A pastor friend of mine once told me that he used to preach an occasional sermon on parenting but no longer does. When I asked him why, he replied, "I became a parent!"

In the area of unconditional love, my parents really came through. I was your typical strong-willed, hardheaded boy. During my teenage years, Mama worried a lot about me. Frustrated and outdone, she would seek advice from my grandmother, and Grandmother invariably responded as a well-seasoned veteran. She told Mama on numerous occasions, "Max is going up fool's hill. He'll come down one day." I did. A few times I came down hard. But my parents were always there to catch me. And never, for a moment, did I ever doubt their love and acceptance. Repeatedly, throughout their lives, they have been there for me. For this I am forever grateful.

Still, I did get three whippin's—twice from Daddy and once from Mama. They were painful. They were shocking. And they were embarrassing (not shaming). However, the most important aspect of my three whippin's was that *they worked*! The message my parents were trying to get across came through loud and clear. After each of my three whippin's, there was not a single thread of confusion left in my young mind. What I did was wrong, and I remembered it for a lifetime. The three lessons I learned from my whippin's were: Don't lie, don't steal, and never ever stick your tongue out at Mama!

Mama whipped me only once, but that's all it took. I can remember as if it were yesterday. I was about five years old, and Mama instructed me to help her clean up my room. With a defiant smirk on my face, I turned to her, stuck out my tongue, and in a most disloyal fashion said, "NO!" A lesson was taught me that day—a lesson that forever changed my attitude. Mama didn't sit me down and try to reason with me. She didn't threaten me with hollow words. No, Mama took action. She tanned my behind with Daddy's belt! Words were few, but the message was loud and clear: "Respect your mother and respect other elders in your life." Now, I'm sure this experience was a much bigger ordeal in my little mind than in my mother's. Knowing my mom and the dear that she is, she probably shocked me more than inflicted pain. Mama couldn't hurt a flea, much less me. She did what she had to do, though, to get my attention. Though the whole ordeal lasted only about ten minutes, the effect lasted a lifetime. To this day when I see kids who are disrespectful to their parents and elders, it annoys me to no end. After my whippin', Mama held me in her arms and assured me that she loved me.

The instant we come out of our mother's womb, all of us are instinctively enrolled into the

School of Life. From our first breath until our last, class is in session. Some of life's lessons are painful; some are not. Some come as a result of our own stupidity; some come through honest mistakes; others come through situations completely out of our control. What we assimilate from these life lessons is the key to enhanced living and realizing our full capacity as a person. Each obstacle that comes our way in life is an opportunity for education and development. When we are young, these life lessons stem from incidents such as sticking our tongue out at Mama or missing the school bus. As we grow older, however, life lessons come from more serious circumstances. The question is: Will we use these opportunities to expand our character, or will we simply pass on unchanged?

I don't consider myself to be a professional counselor by any means. I'm simply an ex-pastor who has learned a great deal from life's school. I've been dealt some hard lessons. Some I created and some were completely out of my control. Personally, I've experienced a devastating divorce, a disabled child, career loss, and financial ruin all before the age of thirty-five. I know what it feels like to hit rock bottom—to be totally broken.

During what I call "my broken years," I was confronted with many choices. I could live in denial, which I did for a great while. I could shift the blame for my difficulties on other people and circumstances. I did that too. I could continue on in my bitterness and self-defeating behavior; or I could stop running, face myself honestly, and admit "I am in need." I needed God. I needed counsel. I needed love and understanding. Eventually I came to the end of myself, and I'm here to say that was the most freeing day of my life. By seeking to learn through my mistakes and circumstances instead of evading them, the worst events in my life became springboards into a much richer and more successful existence.

After my divorce, I stopped blaming the other party and recognized that I had certain characteristics that needed dealing with. If I dealt with those areas, I could experience new life; but if I continued on the present path, I would simply repeat the same self-defeating behavior over and over, with similar results. Since then I've learned how to give and receive love in healthy ways.

My son James has a disability. He is totally deaf. Oh, how I have wished he were not. The pain is ever-present. For nine years, I've prayed for God to heal him. He has not. Instead, I've seen a side of God's grace that I would have never known if an instant healing had occurred. Through the years, I've learned not to view my son as disabled but as gifted. God has given him unique characteristics and abilities. Because of his deafness, he is much more expressive in his personality, which makes him a blessing to be around. Everybody he meets falls in love with him. James is more observant of his surroundings than other kids his age. His deafness allows him to block out distractions and concentrate on important tasks. Because James has had to struggle in certain areas, he has developed an unusual attitude of compassion for others. He is most definitely gifted.

My financial ruin came about through circumstances entirely out of my control. I was doing all the right things—saving, investing, minimizing debt, tithing. Yet the bottom fell out. However, even that has turned around. Being backed into a corner forced me to break out of the security of my comfort zone, trust God, and utilize my creativity. Now I am doing what I've always dreamed of. My heart goes out to those people who are bound to dead-end jobs simply because of security. Am I saying quit? No. Am I saying be unthankful? No. But be alert and open to change. Getting laid off might be the best thing that ever happened to a person. As I look back on my life, I actually thank God for allowing "my broken years."

Og Mandino, one of the greatest motivational teachers of our time, said in the book *Are You Happy?* by Dennis Wholey:

> Sometimes life is very painful. We are filled with negative feelings and there is a sense of hopelessness and despair. We try to deal with hurt. Many of us resort to killing our pain with such substances as alcohol, drugs, pills, or food. Our self-image may be so low that we form unhealthy dependencies not on substances that temporarily make us feel better, but on people who we believe will make our hurt go away. However, the pain becomes greater, and sooner or later we have to take an honest look at the mess we have made of our lives. When we are sick and tired of being sick and tired, we are often motivated to

change. *Human beings are capable of dramatic change; out of the greatest pain frequently comes the greatest change. The quality of life after a remarkable turnabout is amazing.*

Although we may not be aware of it, most of us choose the kind of life we lead. Every day we make choices that determine whether we will be happy or unhappy, be productive or unproductive, grow or stagnate. As life brings us new and different challenges, we make choices that lead, ultimately, to self-defeat or healthy growth.

Basically there are two types of people in the world today. The first we will call the *superficial existers*. These people are all around us, merely existing. They're good at denial. They learn just enough to get by. They continue in their self-defeating behaviors, often oblivious to them or just ignoring them. Theirs is a shallow existence of mere survival. These people go through life never really experiencing true freedom or reaching their potential.

The second we will call *farmers*. Why farmers? Because they are learning and growing, drawing out of life's situations insight, and cultivating a richer life by planting their insight into their daily routines. These people affect others. They have impact and influence—not by elevating themselves but by simply being. They are people of depth.

I saw a story on the national news that grabbed my attention. The story was about a hundred-year-old woman who still works full time as a newspaper editor. She works from 9:00 A.M. to 4:30 P.M. five days a week, writes a weekly column in the paper, and is working on a book. It is an amazing story. At age sixty-five she was let go from the competing newspaper because of company policy. The next day she was hired by the paper across town, and that was thirty-five years ago! She's still going strong. When interviewed, she said that she "views each new day as a learning experience." She continued in a humble mode: "The older I get, the more I realize I have a lot to learn." This woman is a farmer. You would think after a hundred years she would know enough; yet she's still learning and growing. The truth is, when we stop learning and growing, we die. What an example for all of us to follow.

The highway to enhanced living is found more often by people who realistically face

themselves, learn from situations, and take action. All of us, from time to time, vacillate between being a superficial exister and a farmer.
Usually, however, we become farmers when
something traumatic happens to overwhelm our
ability to control life. Our natural tendency is to
drift through life, not dealing with issues or
making the positive changes needed in our daily
situations until we are jolted by an event that
causes us to look honestly at ourselves.

My whippin' from Mama wasn't particularly
fun, but it was necessary to help develop my
character. Life sometimes hands us unpleasant
circumstances. When it does, we can be stub-
born, or we can allow those unpleasant circumstances to be a positive motivation for growth.
While is it important to go through the normal
grieving process, there comes a point in every
adversity, regardless of its intensity, when we
must learn from it and grow. The alternative is
to drown in our own despair. Those who take a
woe-is-me attitude eventually fall behind. Take
on an attitude of learning. Become a farmer.
Seize whatever you can from life's incidents,
both pleasant and unpleasant. Your life will
never be the same.

2
Even Toddlers Do It

A FOUL SMELL FILLED the room. At first I tried to dismiss it. Yet the smell got more and more distinct. "No," I said with a moan. "Not again. It can't be. I thought we were past this stage!" It was true, though, and I had to face the music. Kristen, my two-year-old daughter, had let it go again, without warning, in her pants. Not number one but the dreaded number two. It wasn't like she hadn't been warned about this either. She knew better and had made a conscious choice. Kristen was going through intense potty training, and I was her drill sergeant. When confronted with her transgression, Kristen flat-out denied her actions.

"Kristen, did you poopy in your pants?" I questioned.

"Oh, nooooooo, I didn't poopy in my pants," Kristen replied, shrugging her shoulders.

"Then who do you suppose put that poopy in there?"

Kristen stood still. Thought for a while. Then looked straight up at me with her big, blue eyes and boldly proclaimed, "Daddy did it!" Talk about a major blame shift. Even toddlers do it!

Recently an accountant for one of the oldest and most respected church denominations in America was charged with embezzling several million dollars. Leaders were in complete shock because she had been with the denomination for years and had been deeply trusted. While the embezzlement was taking place, the denomination had to shut down several key ministries due to lack of funds, which made this particular crime even more deplorable. The stolen funds had been filtered through many different sources and took years to track. Obviously a well-developed strategy had been executed. When responding to the charge of embezzlement, the accountant's lawyer read a letter of rebuttal. The letter claimed that the embezzlement occurred due to stress and anguish in the workplace. Can you believe it? How ridiculous!

As humans, our tendency is to blame our own failures on other people or on circumstances. From infancy through adulthood, most of us, from time to time, have become familiar with blame shifting. We claim our distress and difficulty stem from the unreasonable people or unreasonable circumstances around us. The truth is our parents made mistakes. Some of them were even abusive in different ways. Our spouses mess up. The people that we are around daily make serious blunders. If we have been wounded by these people, there's no doubt the pain is real, and their actions are inexcusable. But regardless of what was done to us in the past, we alone are personally responsible for the way we react and how we live.

Until we realize that we alone own our actions—that they are solely ours; that they don't belong to anyone else—we can't hope to resolve our inner conflicts and start having effective relations with those around us. Any psychologist will affirm that going back through our lives to identify root causes for our behavior is not so we can place blame on those who hurt us but so we can make the needed adjustments in our present course.

The reason many of us have a problem with taking personal responsibility is because we view responsibility as "blame" or "fault." However, responsibility actually means the ability to respond. Whatever our dilemma, we all have the ability to respond, and our response can make our condition either better or worse.

Taking personal responsibility involves admitting to our weaknesses, seeking the reason behind them, and then taking the positive steps needed to counter the behavior. This takes humility and maturity. Choosing to remain oblivious to our weaknesses and blaming others when conflict arises shows immaturity and the inability for self-analysis.

PERSONAL RESPONSIBILITY AND GOD

ONE OF THE problems I have seen time and time again in religious circles is that many people go to God with their personal problems, expecting Him to fix everything without any real work on their part. They pray and quote scriptures praising God for His intervention, but that's it. There's no looking in the mirror and saying, "Okay, God, deal with me. Identify the areas in my life that I need to work on."

Jim's wife, Kim, left him after six years of marriage. Obviously they both had some serious problems. I'm not justifying what Kim did, but she had been trying to get Jim's attention for years. However, he was so caught up in himself and his way of doing things that he never quite got the message until she actually filed for divorce. When she did file, Jim was blown out of the water. "How could she do this to me and our family?" he cried. Kim wrote him letters telling why she filed and what he could do to possibly reconcile things. She wanted the marriage to work out. But Jim could not face the fact that he did anything wrong—that he needed to change. So he ran to his mama and daddy; and, instead of telling him what he needed to hear, they shifted all blame to Kim. She was terrible. She needed to get her act together. Then Jim started going to church. He brought home a Bible and told Kim that God wanted to heal their marriage. Of course, what

Jim wanted was for Kim to come back and accept things as they were. But Kim's view of a healed marriage was a husband who would admit his mistakes. Jim prayed and preached to Kim for months but never took any personal responsibility to change. Jim didn't ask what he could do to restore the relationship, or try to win Kim back. He failed to accept responsibility for any aspect of the breakup. Kim went ahead with the divorce. Jim got angry at God and dropped out of church. The real tragedy is that Jim is still blaming Kim and God for his personal failure, and he is doomed to repeat the same pattern again if he does not get help.

Does God want to heal relationships? Of course He does, and He will. I've seen God restore sons and fathers, daughters and mothers, husbands and wives, and friendships over and over again. God is in the restoration business. But He will not do our part, and we do have a big part to play in our personal healing and in the healing of our relationships.

I am an outdoor enthusiast. On any given Saturday you can find me hiking through the woods. A while back I was hiking along some rocky cliffs that had a cool river running between them. A bridge crossed the river, but the cliffs and the bridge ran together so it appeared there was no way to get down to the river. The cliffs were not that high—maybe thirty feet, but they were steep and unclimbable without any gear. My heart was set on the river, though, and I was determined to get down there. So I slid down as far as I could, and then I jumped. It was crazy, I know. I made a calculated risk and jumped. After scouting the situation, I was certain that the place I would land would be safe. Plus, I was taught how to land and roll safely in a rappeling course. I viewed it as a challenge. The jump was a success. As soon as my feet hit the ground, though, a thought hit me. "How am I going to get back up?" Getting down was the easy part. Getting back up was going to take a miracle. But I was down there, so I decided to enjoy the river for a while. I played in the river for about an hour and realized I had better start heading back and figure out how to get back up. As I walked and thought about it, the more I realized the seriousness of my situation. I started to get scared. I prayed a simple prayer to God. "Lord, please help!" Then an amazing thing happened. I looked down, and I'm telling the truth, there was a long nylon rope just lying there. In the middle of nowhere. It was just lying there as if someone knew I was going to need it. I couldn't believe it! Obviously someone had left it there, but I saw it as a miracle!

As I approached the bridge, I started calculating how to best utilize the rope. Then another thought hit me. "Yes, you have a rope. Yes, you have a way out, but this is not going to be easy." For what seemed like an eternity I tried to find a way to throw the rope so it would catch on the bridge or a rock or something so I could pull myself up. Finally I found a little crack in the wall of the bridge, about an inch wide. I tied a knot on the rope, and after a lot of tries, the rope slid in the crack. Thankfully, the knot held it there. Relief. But still I had to climb the rope. Because I was climbing up the bridge, I had nowhere to put my feet for leverage. The rope was just hanging down in the air. Have you ever tried to climb a twenty-foot rope in midair? It's not easy. It took all the strength I had just to make it to the top of the bridge. When I finally made it up, my shouts of jubilation echoed throughout the canyon.

While pondering this incident, I saw some

striking parallels between it and our personal lives. Before I could get out of the canyon, first I had to admit that I made a huge error in judgment. Then I had to take some steps to change the situation. One step was prayer. God provided a rope. But then I had to do my part. And it was hard work. God did not send an angel to lift me out of the canyon. He did not climb the rope for me. What He did was provide a way out, but it was up to me to utilize His provision.

In our personal lives God often gives us just enough rope to climb out of the dark holes we are experiencing. Yet if we don't take personal responsibility in practical ways and work hard, we will continue to live in darkness and repeat our self-destructive patterns.

3

Monsters Under the Bed

MOST OF US can remember as young children calling out to Mom or Dad in the middle of the night because we thought monsters were hiding under our bed or in our closet. The fear was so real we could testify that we actually saw the monsters moving. Our parents turned on the hall light, rushed to our side, and assured us it was just a shadow from an outside tree or light pole or something. A soothing word, a light left on, and our fear was put to rest. As time passed, we grew and soon found ourselves facing even bigger fears. I'll never forget the empty, sickening feeling in my stomach as I timidly stepped on the school bus for the first time.

I pressed my cheeks to the window and watched Mom until the bus turned at the end of the block. Though that seemed an overwhelming fear at that time, once again with the help of my parents, it was dealt with; and soon going to school became second nature.

A large portion of growing up is learning to confront our fears and deal with them. The older we get, however, the more powerful our fears can become. As we add years to our lives and move into adulthood, our fears no longer stem from boogiemen or school buses. Instead, they arise from past negative experiences, and like any other disorder, they come in many varieties caused by a myriad of reasons: divorce (either parental or from one's own spouse), death of a loved one, family history of disease, loss of a job, pressures to succeed, childhood abuse, and so on. These types of experiences can produce dominant feelings of fear that can immobilize a person's ability to experience life. All too often we carry these unresolved fears into our relationships. Undoubtedly, fear is a real and present force. It keeps us from seizing opportunities, tears down our vitality for living, and prevents us from developing healthy relation-

ships. Yet fear is manageable and need not dom-
inate us. Do not believe for a moment that you
must live with fear. You don't. But overcoming
fear is a long-term process that demands self-
discipline and commitment.

FOUR-POINT PLAN FOR MANAGING FEAR

*1. Understand the difference between healthy and
unhealthy fear.*
Healthy fear is essential. It is a tool fashioned
by God for our protection. An absence of it
would create a deficiency in our personality
causing a shortage of common sense. Healthy
fear keeps us from doing hazardous and sense-
less things.

Recently our community suffered a tragic
loss. A nineteen-year-old boy and two of his
friends were killed in an automobile accident.
He was driving his car so fast that he lost control and hit a tree head-on. The police confirmed that he was going well over 100 mph.
Most of the people who knew this young man
also knew he had an attitude. I'm not sure the

exact model of his car, but it was a real hot rod. One of his girlfriends being interviewed on the local news said she had ridden with him at speeds up to 150 mph. He was hot. He was arrogant. He had a sticker on his car that read in big bold letters NO FEAR. He is now dead. His epitaph could read NO FEAR, NO RESPECT, NOW DEAD. It's a tragic story. This young man could have used a dose of healthy fear.

Unhealthy fear, on the other hand, chips away at our self-worth. It fills our life with obsessions and drains us of strength. Jordan and Margaret Paul give an excellent description of unhealthy fear in their book *Do I Have to Give Up Me to Be Loved By You:*

> Imagine yourself living in a swamp. You know that swamp inch by inch, every safe path, every danger spot. All your life you pick your way around the swamp eking out a bare existence. You can just make out, along the borders of the swamp, a cleaner, brighter, shinier world, but you do not venture into it. Passersby make fun of you; friends urge you to get out of your rut and taste the better life that is possible. You see

the logic of their arguments and the ridiculousness of your choice, but you fail every time you try to leave.

Becoming more and more depressed, you sink lower and lower into the muck and gloom of your world. Then one day, someone new stops to chat and says to you, "Living this way seems stupid, but there must be something very important keeping you here."

"Oh, no," you protest, "I'm just a jerk."

Your new-found friend persists, "What is there outside of this place that you are afraid of?"

"Well, I don't know, but I imagine there's a big hole with demons in it that I might step into."

"What makes you think so?"

"I fell in holes as a child and got hurt a lot."

"Oh, now it begins to make sense."

"Yes, it does. Maybe I'm not such a jerk after all."

Unhealthy fear keeps us in the swamps of life, bogged down, unable to move forward.

2. Pinpoint your unhealthy fears.

The person in the swamp pinpointed his fear. He had been injured as a child by falling into holes. This wasn't a cure, but it was the first step in getting out of the swamp. To overcome our fear, it is imperative that we determine exactly what generates the feeling of fear in us. This is not always an easy task. Because fear manifests itself in so many different forms, it is vital that we find the root cause. Initial diagnoses are usually mere symptoms of a much deeper fear. Discovering root fears means diving below the surface of our emotions and digging around, which can be a painful process.

Let's take Ted, for example. Growing up, all through high school and college, Ted never had a date. He didn't go to the prom or anything like that. He was nice looking, intelligent, and had a lot to offer. Yet he continually battled with problems of low self-esteem. He liked women but could never get the courage to ask one out. Because he was such an introvert, he never allowed himself to be in a position even to meet women. Ted was over thirty-three before he finally got the courage to ask someone out. Whenever Ted was confronted about this, he would say he was just shy or had a hard time meeting new people. The truth was that Ted suffered from a deep fear of rejection. But his fear of rejection was only a surface diagnosis. The root cause of his fear went all the way back to his early childhood. When Ted was only five years old, his dad and mom divorced. His mom left his dad because he was an alcoholic and physically and verbally abusive. Ted's mother remarried, and he was raised by a loving stepfather. However, deep wounds were embedded in his heart. As he grew, Ted never dealt with his emotional pain. To survive he simply pushed his pain deeper and deeper into his subconscious. All through childhood and adolescence, Ted felt he never quite fit in with the rest of the family. He never saw his natural dad again, and his mother and stepfather had two children of their own, which left Ted feeling even more like an outcast. For thirty-six years Ted carried this emotional baggage; but because it had been buried for so long, the fears and insecurities simply became a part of his personality. Finally Ted married. Now his fears and insecurities are negatively affecting his marriage. For himself and for the sake of his family, Ted must get a grip on his fears. The only way he will be free is to go back to his childhood and dig up the roots of his fear. Then he must sever them by applying truth to the lies he's believed about himself. It won't be easy, but it is the only way he can be free from the chains that bind him.

Not all of us have the deep emotional baggage that Ted had, but the process is the same. We have to pinpoint the root cause of our fear. Note that we must dig up and identify the roots of our fear *not* to shift blame for our problems but to help us to sever them and move forward. After we have done so, we can turn to step 3.

3. Apply truth to your root fear.
The apostle John proclaimed, "You will know the truth, and the truth shall set you free." When dealing with our fears, this holds added significance. Once we understand the truth about ourselves and our situations, we can sever root fears. All unhealthy fear results from believing lies about ourselves and situations.

The person living in the swamp was bound there because he actually believed holes with demons existed. Truth frees people. Yet often it is difficult to accept truth when we have believed a lie for so long. But what is truth?

There are three simple but profound truths that, if applied to our root fears, will transform our lives. However, they must become a part of us, and that will require time and work.

The first truth is: *We are people of worth.* The lie is that somehow we don't measure up to those around us—that we are not valuable assets to the world. Ted had been carrying false guilt and shame around all of his life. Like the person in the swamp who believed in demon-filled holes, Ted, because of the abusive actions of his father, believed he was not worthy of true love and acceptance. His father told him lies. His father made him feel ashamed and guilty. But was this warranted? No. The ultimate truth is God's word, and God demonstrated we are people of worth by sending Jesus Christ to die for us. Think about it. We are so important that the God of the universe died for us. This truth transcends lies. It transcends what people do or say to us. It is a higher law. Ted's father may have instilled numerous lies, such as "You're no good. You're stupid." But St. Paul says, "Who dares accuse us whom God has chosen for his own? Will God? No! He is the one who has forgiven us and given us right standing with Himself" (Romans 8:33). Ted's father may have said, "I wish you were never born." But God says, "Before you were born I knew you and loved you" (Psalm 139:13–15). God creates us, loves us, and that gives us worth.

The second truth is: *We have the power within us to make a stand against our fears.* Saint Timothy said that God has given us a spirit of power and love—not fear. God has imparted to each of us the power within to stand up to our fears and deal with them. If it is a person we're afraid of we must face him or her. If it is a situation, we must confront it. We must tackle our fears, whatever they are, head-on, with God's power, if we are to have freedom in our lives. The lie is "I can't." The truth is, God has given us the power to overcome.

The third truth is: *Love defeats fear.* Love is one of the most misused words in the English language. It has been made synonymous with Hollywood's portrayal of lustful sex. But love has little to do with Hollywood's version. Love is a strong, powerful force that crushes fear. About fifteen years ago one of my best friends and I went to the beach. While we were there, we saw a man hit a woman and knock her to the ground. My friend moved to stop the man. When he did, five or six other men, all buddies of this guy, jumped on my friend. They had him on the ground and were beating him severely. I was watching the whole ordeal. I knew I had to do something. But what? I couldn't let them kill my friend. Fear raced through my mind. I began to shake. But then, almost subconsciously, I found myself running and diving into the pile of fists. I pulled one man up by the hair and punched him, pulled another and punched him, grabbed my friend, and we both sprinted to the car and sped away. In that situation, love for my friend overruled my fear. I've experienced this sensation several times in my life. With my wife and children, I often find a supernatural courage arises in me to protect them in certain situations. There is no fear in love because real love casts out fear. Ultimately, it is God's perfect love in us that can crush our fears, whatever they may be.

4. Take action now.
Action cures fear. Remember this principle and it will change your life. *Action cures fear.* Pinpoint your fear, learn the truth, and then take action. An amazing thing happened when I rescued my friend. I was terrified before I took action. But as soon as I made the decision and started run-

ning, the fear was literally replaced with a sense of power. This principle is true within any area where we are experiencing fear. Salesmen are taught that the first call of the day is the most important. Why? Because it's the hardest. Once that first call is made, the second one is easier. The temptation for a salesman is to sit around all morning and sip coffee, putting it off, instead of getting out there. Hesitation and procrastination always amplify fear. Action always reduces fear.

Do not give in to the lie that you have to live with your fears. It's not true. With God's help you can defeat your fears.

Remember:

1. Understand the difference between healthy and unhealthy fear.

2. Pinpoint your unhealthy fears.

3. Apply truth to your root fear.

4. Take action now.

4

Barking
at the
Coach's Wife

HAVE YOU EVER said something stupid? You know, spoken before you thought — verbally leaped into a situation before you looked it over. Once, when trying to make conversation, I asked a woman when her baby was due. Guess what? She wasn't pregnant! Take my advice. Don't ever do that, unless you really get a charge from feeling like a heel.

That was nothing, however. The mother of all stupid things I did with my tongue was tell a woman at a football game, "A blind man could see that the Panthers need a new coach. There is no way any team can possibly be that bad," I barked arrogantly. "It's clear that the coach doesn't know what he is doing." You guessed it. She was the coach's wife! I was barking at the coach's wife! Of all the hundreds of people sitting in the bleachers, I had to unload my colossal knowledge of football on the coach's wife. She was sitting in the stands with her three children just like all the rest of the spectators. How was I supposed to know who she was? Needless to say, she was not a happy camper.

But wait, it gets worse. I was pastoring at the time and had gone to the game with a family from our church whose son was playing. As my luck had it, this family was close friends with the coach and his family and had on several occasions invited them to our church. In fact, the two wives worked together. So not only did I offend the coach's wife and children, but I had offended the family I had gone with. Humiliated and nauseated best described my state.

Even pastors can mess up big time! It's easy to laugh now. Trust me, though, I wasn't laughing then. To try to salvage what little respect I had left, I sent a letter of apology to both the coach's wife and the family that attended our church. Notice, I said attended—past tense. They soon discontinued their membership. The letter helped somewhat, but it was not enough to recover the hurt and embarrassment my tongue had caused.

Ever since kindergarten we have been taught the old adage "Sticks and stones may break my bones, but words can never hurt me." Don't believe it. It's not true. Words have power. They have the power to encourage, create, transform, or hurt, tear, and destroy.

Recently while watching a television talk show, I saw a young woman who had lost over 200 pounds. Sitting on the stage was this beautiful woman who looked like a model. When the before-and-after pictures of her were revealed, I was stunned. It was almost inconceivable that the woman onstage was the same woman in the pictures. As the show progressed, she talked about how she accomplished her goal and what motivated her. Then the host introduced a young man, an acquaintance of hers, who had no idea why he was invited on the show. The woman wanted to thank him for what he had done for her. He, puzzled, was not aware of what he did to help.

She then began to disclose the story. She started by saying that losing the first 20 pounds was the most difficult. It had been so difficult that she felt losing 200 pounds would be impossible. After losing her first 20 pounds, she decided to go to her high school prom in the hope someone would notice her. In her mind, however, she had already decided to quit dieting. At the prom no one danced with her or had anything to do with her. She was fighting back tears, thinking suicidal thoughts, when this young man spoke to her. All he did was tell her she looked nice and asked her if she had lost weight. According to her, he was a gentleman and treated her as a person with dignity. His few positive comments so touched her broken spirit that it encouraged her to reach deep inside and continue pursuing her goal. After the prom, they graduated and went separate ways until the show some three years later. It took her almost three years to lose 200 pounds. Now that she had accomplished her goal, she wanted him to see her and know how he had motivated her.

What an amazing story! Think about the power of those few encouraging words. Now think what might have occurred if this struggling young woman had received negative words that night. Instead of her broken spirit being mended, it would have been crushed. And the profound thing is the young man had not a clue of how transforming his words had been. Words are powerful! Benjamin Franklin wrote in 1740, "Man's tongue is soft, and bone doth lack; yet a stroke therewith may break a man's back."

Helen Yglesias's brother's words broke her spirit. When Helen was a teenager during the Great Depression, she aspired to be a writer. She started writing a book and was excited about it. She eagerly let her brother read her manuscript, expecting encouragement and even a bit of constructive criticism. But his response almost destroyed Helen. "Nobody in the world is going to be interested in that &$#@* stuff you're writing," he said brashly. "You'd have to be a genius to get away with this boring stuff, and you're no genius." Frustrated and hurt, Helen ripped her manuscript to shreds. Those words, spoken by her insensitive brother, caused a forty-year delay in Helen Yglesias's writing career. Her brother had convinced her that writing was a waste of time. But after that long delay, Helen couldn't take it anymore and, with the constant encouragement of a friend, finally wrote her book. The book became a best-seller and she went on to write many other best-sellers, such as *Family Feeling, Sweetsir, Starting Early, Anew, Over and Late,* which have made her a highly respected author.

The power of words can inspire. They also can crush. Solomon put it another way: "Death and life are in the power of the tongue" (Proverbs 18:21).

5

Risky Business

On August 19, 1859, 50,000 spectators huddled around the misty edges of the Niagara Falls. They came from near and far for one reason—to watch a young daredevil by the name of Emelé Blondin. Blondin had announced to the world he would walk across the unruly Niagara Falls on a rope only two inches in diameter— something no one in history had ever attempted. This spectacular feat would take Blondin from the American border to the Canadian border suspended 160 feet in the air. One false step would leave the Frenchman shattered on the jagged rocks that lined the river.

Almost effortlessly, though, Blondin accomplished his goal. When he reached the Canadian border, the crowd was chanting "Blondin! Blondin! Blondin!" Yet Blondin's act was far from over. That day he danced on the rope, pushed a wheelbarrow over it, and even crossed it blindfolded! All were indeed remarkable feats. However, it was Blondin's last act that stunned the world.

Blondin faced the crowd and boldly asked them, "I wish to go across one last time, except this time with someone on my shoulders. Do you believe that I can?" Instantly the crowd voiced their approval. "You can! We believe!" they cheered. Seeing the crowd's enthusiastic response, Blondin requested that someone step out from them as a volunteer.

A blanket of silence dropped over the crowd. The rumble of the falls intensified. Minutes seemed like days. "Surely no one in his right mind would actually volunteer," some muttered. Others placed bets. Then just before the crowd gave way to disbelief, one man by the name of Harry Colcord stepped out to volunteer. Blondin gallantly placed Colcord on his shoulders, and they surged across the massive falls, rewriting history with every step.

. . .

Although walking a tightrope across the Niagara Falls was staggering when it involved just
Blondin, the event was simply a daredevil per-
forming. Over the years we've come to expect
this sort of activity from daredevils. However,
when Harry Colcord stepped on the scene, the
story became much more engrossing. A professional daredevil taking a risk is one thing, but a
spectator getting on his back is quite another.
Colcord had to place total trust in Blondin. He
knew that once he was dangling over the mighty
Niagara there would be no turning back. He
also knew that if Blondin slipped, they would
both be dead men. On the other hand, Blondin
had to trust Colcord as well. Blondin didn't
know if Colcord was going to wiggle and throw
him off balance or do something stupid that
would cause them to fall. Both men entered into
a mutual relationship of trust high on the ropes.
That's what makes this story so remarkable.

The average human being would never consider doing what Harry Colcord did. Nor would
they attempt to bungee-jump off a moving helicopter, or climb a 5,000-foot cliff free-handed
with no ropes attached. Why? Because the risks

are too absurd. Most people have at least a trifle of common sense. Nevertheless, we are all people of risk. Merely existing in today's society causes us to encounter remarkable odds every day. Consider some of the risks we will face during our lifetime:

Be a victim of a violent crime: 1 in 3.
Die in an auto accident: 1 in 45.
Die of heart disease: 1 in 3.
Die of cancer: 1 in 5.
Die in an airplane crash: 1 in 4,000.
Receive an injury at home this year requiring medical attention: 1 in 13.
Have a disabling accident at home: 1 in 81.
Be murdered: 1 in 95.
Be accidentally poisoned this year: 1 in 100.*

While these risks do not hold the same intensity as Colcord's, we do face them every day; and some of the odds are not very encouraging. Yet to most of us this is not a new revelation.

---

* All of these statistics are documented in *The Book of Risks* by Larry Laudan, Ph.D. Copyright 1994. Reprinted by permission of John Wiley & Sons, Inc.

Risk plays a common role in our modern world. It seems as if almost every year someone compiles another study on some new danger we face. But we don't shut down our lives. We don't stay inside all day, give up driving, or stop eating. Most of us accept these risks, take the necessary precautions, and go about living the best we can. The risk of heart disease is decreased by eating right and exercising. Auto fatalities are reduced by wearing seat belts, by not drinking and driving, by being defensive, and by keeping our cars in good condition. A sense of security from crime comes from staying away from bad parts of town, by installing alarms and locks, and by learning self-defense. But even with all these precautions, we still cannot eliminate all our risks. Yet life must go on—and it does.

If we face risks such as these on a daily basis and go on living, why is it that literally millions of us are paralyzed when it comes to taking emotional risks with other people—risks such as revealing our true selves, developing deep friendships, or attempting to love? The answer is not a simple one, but it is clear. We have been wounded . . . abandoned . . . abused. . . .

And we never want to feel that kind of pain again. So, consciously or subconsciously, we protect ourselves. We build barriers that keep our emotions in and others out.

Now understand, protecting our emotion is not a bad thing, when we keep it in balance. We should learn to guard ourselves, but not so well that our natural growth patterns are stifled. If we are involved in a serious automobile accident, for example, usually we learn something from our mistake or the mistake of someone else, get a little bit wiser, and then get back in the driver's seat. In relationships we experience accidents. After they occur, we must learn two lessons if we are going to live healthy lives:

1. Learn something from our mistake so we don't repeat the same mistake again.

2. After taking sufficient time to heal, get back in the driver's seat.

While publishing and editing *Enhance Magazine,* a magazine dealing with emotional issues, I encountered many people who had been hurt in the past by parents, friends, or spouses, and even some who have indicated disappointment with God or the church. These negative experiences have left them disillusioned with future relationships. I can't tell you how many times I've heard statements like: "All men are jerks." "I'll never open up and trust anyone again." "How could Christians be so cruel?"

I was visiting a woman one day and recommended that she start seeking out and building some close friendships. Her response to me was "You'll never know how many times I've been hurt by people." Because of those hurtful experiences, she determined simply not to have close friends anymore. It's tragic but common. Because of bad experiences, we close up, build walls, and move through life unfulfilled and discontent. We prejudge future relationships based on our past. When this occurs, not only are we hindering our own growth, but we are limiting others by putting them in our emotional boxes. The truth is some men are jerks, but a lot are not. The church has its share of hypocrites, but it is also full of many wonderful people. And though you must be cautious, you can trust again. Finding genuine security, being confident, and knowing true love and fulfillment require taking risks. There is no other way. Our lives improve only when we take chances. Leading marriage and family counselor Marian Wood wrote in "The Challenge to Be Yourself," an article that appeared in *Enhance Magazine:*

> The sad thing is that when we "protect" ourselves in this way, we are locking ourselves in a prison of loneliness and stifled growth. . . . There is no way one can experience healthy relationships and completely avoid any risk of being hurt. We keep trying to find ways to elude the risks. Naturally, it makes sense to assess the situation carefully and realistically, and not lay your heart on the line if there are no indications of a positive response. Nevertheless, there is a point at which, if you want to experience healthy relationships, you have to take the bungee jump of love. . . .

Taking chances doesn't mean being stupid, though. After reading about Blondin and Harry Colcord, did you ask yourself how or why? How could Harry Colcord step out and trust like he did? Why would he do such a thing? Well, there is a part of the story I haven't told you. When researching it, I didn't find out until the end either. The whole thing was staged. Harry Colcord was Blondin's manager and was planted in the crowd to look like a spectator. Even so, it was still a risk. According to history, the act had not been rehearsed. Colcord had never done it before—even in practice. Yet it was a minimized risk. He undoubtedly knew what Blondin could do. Colcord had watched him day after day in training and had built a certain level of trust in him. He had spent time with Blondin when the other spectators had not.

We need not open up to just anyone or put our hearts on the ropes only to be stomped on. Having effective relationships involves wisdom and time. Ask questions. Get answers. Is this a relationship that is faithful in the little things? Is it good for me? Does it cause me to compromise my convictions? You get the picture. Get the facts. Don't be foolish. But go for it! Mark Twain once remarked:

> We should be careful to get out of an experience only the wisdom that is in it— and stop there; lest we be like the cat that

sits down on a hot-stove lid. She will never sit down on a hot-stove lid again, and that is well; but also she will never sit down on a cold one any more either.

6
What an Incredible Thought!

JOE MONTANA . . . Mr. Rogers . . . Mercedes . . . Volkswagen . . . Laurel . . . Hardy . . . wife . . . Me . . . We all have something in common—a single thread that deeply connects us. We are exceptionally different. I don't mean kinda, sorta different either. I'm talking black and white, cold and hot, elephant and mouse. Think about it. Could you picture Mr. Rogers quarterbacking the 49ers? Or Joe Montana singing "Would you be my neighbor?" I don't think so.

My wife Alanna is a calm, levelheaded introvert. I'm a hyper, adventurous extrovert. I like to travel. I love airports and visting places like New York City and San Francisco. I like it where the people are. She doesn't care to travel much and prefers our quaint little home in the country. I never meet a stranger. She's perfectly content being a stranger. But guess what? We desperately need each other. I think God planned it that way. We are as different as peanut butter and jelly. Yet together we make a dynamic sandwich. She helps keep me in check, and I help her experience new things. We are good for each other. In his book *Power Thoughts*, Robert Schuller affirms this sentiment:

> I am a conceptual person. My wife of well over forty years is pragmatic. I get the dreams and ideas. She instantly perceives the challenges, the problems, and the difficulties involved in the proposal. She is pragmatic. I am conceptual. Power thinkers see the conceptual and the pragmatic as complementary—not conflicting. Because my wife sees the potential problems, obstacles and difficulties, and I see the fantastic possibilities, we simply join hearts and heads in a paradigm to strategize success.

What an incredible thought! God created each of us unique with distinct abilities; and we are all, in some way, interconnected with each other. No man is an island unto himself. No one person has the corner on all truth. To think so is a delusion. Bruce Barton, the author and historian, said, "If you have anything really valuable to contribute to the world, it will come through the expression of your own personality—that single spark of divinity that sets you off and makes you different from every other living creature." Recognizing and appreciating our own uniqueness, along with the uniqueness of others, is a major step toward effective living.

Notes

7

Difficult People

DIFFICULT PEOPLE. JERKS. Frustration. Hurt. Irritation. Annoyance. Enough said. End of chapter . . . not! But if I did end the chapter here, I bet it would still help a lot of folks. Many would read those first few words, take a deep breath, and say, "Whew, thank God somebody out there understands."

All of us—or at least the large majority of us—live in situations where we must interact with difficult people on a regular basis. If you don't, start counting your blessings right now! They're out there, all around, and they can make our lives miserable. They're in our fami-

lies (most commonly), our jobs, and even our
churches and synagogues.

Difficult people, for our purposes, are those
individuals in our lives who, because of their
temperament, cause us untold agony. They have
the uncanny knack for saying hurtful things,
pronouncing judgment, never admitting they're
wrong, being controlling and manipulating, and
seeing others' blind spots clearly, yet remaining
oblivious to their own. They always have the
inside track on the truth. These people don't
just insult our intelligence, they wound us—
sometimes leaving lifelong scars. Author Joyce
Landorf calls them "irregular people." Listen to
what she says about them in her book *Irregular
People:*

> I'm sure that much of the time irregular
> people have no idea of the continual hurts
> inflicted by the darts they hurl. Sometimes
> they do know, but can't (or won't) stop the
> verbal or nonverbal abuse. . . .
>
> Irregular people don't merely "bug"
> us—they wound, stab, pull out chunks of
> our heart, and the poison darts hit deeper
> as the relationship continues. Verbal and

nonverbal abuse leave invisible scars and a feeling of emptiness that is as big as the Grand Canyon.

Normally a commencement ceremony is not the most stimulating of events, but there are exceptions. I attended one as I was writing this chapter. Wouldn't you know, the guest speaker spoke about a difficult person whose cruelty he had to overcome. The speaker was a famous doctor who, for a period of time, had worked in the emergency room at Johns Hopkins University Hospital.

One night a woman came in who had been stabbed forty-seven times yet was still breathing. She was hanging on to life by a thread. The main function of the ER doctor, he recounted, was to get the patient as stable as possible before surgery. This doctor and his technicians worked intensely to stabilize her condition. He explained that they poured out their soul in an all-out effort to save this woman. It worked. She survived the emergency room and was wheeled into surgery. Remarkably, she survived surgery as well.

When it was over, the surgeon, who also was

a hospital director, in front of everyone, arrogantly took credit for saving the woman's life and then brazenly criticized the ER doctor and his team saying that the patient had degenerated while under their care. This was typical of this guy. He was a real jerk, and everyone knew it. Still, though, the team was deflated; and the ER doctor, our speaker, was deeply wounded because he and the team had really given their all. Associating on a daily basis with this surgeon/director made work at times miserable, and it took the speaker years to recover from some of the negative actions and comments that this man had made. We will see later in the chapter, however, that this difficult person was used as a motivational force to push the ER doctor to greatness.

Difficult people can be parents, in-laws, bosses, or coworkers—sometimes even a spouse. They are typically people who are permanent fixtures in our routine. This is one of the reasons why difficult people are so difficult. They are not mere acquaintances. We can't just get away from them, as we can the rude people we come across daily at the supermarket and elsewhere. No, we are forced, due to circumstances, to interact with them frequently. When we do interact with them, often our hypersensitivity complicates the situation. We respond to them by making abrupt replies, usually out of character, making us seem even more vulnerable; by becoming defensive rather than focusing on the issue at hand; by taking their critical comments too personally; or by withdrawing completely. These are all natural but ineffective responses that diminish our chances of transforming a negative encounter into a positive one.

The remainder of this chapter focuses on how we can have positive encounters with the difficult people in our lives. Before we proceed any further, it must be known that I am an optimistic person. There is power in optimism. In dealing with difficult people, however, you cannot win, no matter what. I repeat, you cannot win with these people. So right now, sit back, take another deep breath, and get out of your system the notion that you can somehow impress them or change them. It's not going to happen. At least, you're not going to be the one to do it — maybe God will, but that's His call, not ours. You don't impress or change these people. You deal with them—on their level. They can sniff out insecurity like a shark sniffs blood. The only way you can have a positive encounter with difficult people is to be secure in who you are as a person. You see, difficult people always have to be in a one-up position. They always have to be on top or in control. This is a subconscious, inherent need. They cannot allow themselves to be in a position that is not on top. It's beyond them to do so. They are literally incapable. We'll discuss why a little later.

So, how do we deal with these difficult people? How do we change negative encounters into positive ones? Have you ever heard the old saying, "If it's going to be, it's up to me"? There are four simple keys that, when applied, can, over time (it won't happen overnight), begin to transform our negative encounters into positive ones. It is up to us; our difficult people are not going to help.

1. Keep things in perspective.
The key to everything is how we see. Do you remember when we were kids, in the back of comic books were those advertisements for X-ray glasses? Man, how I wanted a pair of

those! Ah, to see secretly through walls, doors, or Holly's dress at school—the ultimate experience for a sixth grader. Suppose we actually could buy a pair of those glasses, and every time we looked at our difficult person, instead of seeing his underwear, we could see beyond the surface into his soul. In most cases we would be surprised, maybe even shocked, at what lies there underneath all the hardness.

Most difficult people have a reason for being difficult. They weren't born difficult. They grew into the role. It was cultivated over a lifetime. Very few people are just jerks. People who are overly critical or hard usually have a severe lack of self-esteem. More often than not, the cause for their excess criticism isn't another person's inferiority, but rather their own feelings of inadequacy. The list of root causes for their inferiority is long: belittled constantly while growing up, shamed for things out of their control, unreasonable expectations put upon them, physical and emotional abuse, early death of a parent, and so on. You get the picture. This is why they must be in a one-up position. The way they feed their self-esteem is by putting others down. As long as they are on top, or in control, in their mind they are okay. As humbling as it may seem, it really has very little to do with us or whether our difficult person likes or loves us. In many cases, our difficult person is a loved one whom we love dearly and who dearly loves us.

As we begin to see difficult people through these X-ray glasses, our attitude toward them starts to change. Oh, the harsh comments still hurt, but not quite as much. The resentment seems to ease a bit because we understand that it's not us they're really upset with. Basically, they are discontented people who are upset with themselves.

2. *Be wise, protect, and sift.*

After we have put key #1 into action, we start feeling pretty good. Things start looking up. We begin to reason, "Hey, the situation might not be quite as grim as once perceived." Be alert, though. Walk cautiously. Protect yourself. I can't tell you how many times I've had a fairly good conversation with my difficult person, and then, boom, I get all excited. Thoughts go through my mind like "Maybe we can have a normal relationship." "I'm confident now." "I have the situation under control." Eagerly I then open up and disclose something really close to my heart, only to once again be shot down. Rat-tat-tat, like an enemy aircraft I plummet smoldering to the ground and crash.

Because of this recurring experience, I've learned, out of necessity, to be wise, protect, and sift. Being wise means learning to read the situation. Your difficult person might be in a bad mood, tired, or irritated. If so, back off. Try to feel where he is emotionally before interacting.

To protect yourself means just that. Just because you are trying to work on your relationship doesn't mean you have to be buddies. In some situations—with a family member, for example—you may desire a deep relationship. But for your own protection and well-being, it is not wise to get too close. Remember, the person's inability to have a healthy relationship with you is based on circumstances out of his or her control. Most difficult people have very few close friends or confidants. It's sad, but they are responsible for their own actions. Help is available to them if they choose it. Dr. David Schwartz wrote in *The Magic of Thinking Big:*

Be extra, extra cautious about this: don't let negative-thinking people—negators—

destroy you. Opinions of these people can be poison. Develop a defense against them. . . .

Don't be rude, or holier than thou, but develop some safe common sense boundaries. Opening wide just asking to be cut to shreds is not wise.

To sift is to develop the knack of taking in the good, profitable information and throwing out the bad. While in graduate school, one of my professors taught me the principle of sifting. Dr. Grizzle always said, "When you are eating a fish and you come to a bone, what do you do? You don't throw out the fish. You throw away the bone and keep eating the meat." Those words have rung true to me numerous times down through the years, and they come in handy when dealing with difficult people. Often these difficult people are all too aware of our weak spots. They can try to manipulate us by using this information. Because of this, it is not always easy to sift out the good from the bad. Nevertheless, through our X-ray glasses we have to at least try to filter the good and throw out the bad.

3. God uses difficult people.

You may not like this one. Some of us are familiar with the scripture, "As iron sharpens iron, so one man sharpens another" (Proverbs 27:17). I believe one of the reasons God does not change certain difficult people and allows them to do their thing is because when we interact with them, often we are forced to take a deeper look at ourselves. This does not mean their actions are excusable. They are not. The ideal way to sharpen one another is through constructive criticism and positive reinforcement — not tearing down. Nonetheless, God uses difficult people if we allow Him to, but He often uses them in a way that is foreign to them. Most of the time they are not aware of how God is using them. God uses them to teach us patience, forgiveness, dependence on Him, and self-examination.

In addition, God uses difficult people to motivate us. Remember the story earlier in this chapter about the emergency room doctor? Later in his speech he told how the negative words of his surgeon/director colleague had so ruffled him that he was inspired to develop a new type of surgeon's tool, which eventually changed the face of surgery. Documentation has shown that over 10,000 lives have been saved because of this device. He credits his motivations to this colleague who made his life miserable. Every time he was put down and told it couldn't be done, he dug a little deeper and was a little more determined.

4. *Judge yourself first.*

Fact: We all have the potential for being difficult people. Fact: We all have, at one time or another, been someone's difficult person. "Why do you look at the speck of sawdust in your brother's eye and pay no attention to the plank in your own eye? How can you say to your brother, 'Let me take the speck out of your eye,' when all the time there is a plank in your own eye? You hypocrite, first take the plank out of your own eye, and then you will see clearly to remove the speck from your brother's eye" (Matthew 7:3–5). Before we become too hasty in judgment against our difficult person, it is critical that we recognize that we all have the potential of being difficult people. Looking inside ourselves first and understanding that we too fall short helps us develop an attitude of meekness instead of hostility. Also, notice the scripture did not say to ignore our brother's problem, but rather to judge ourselves first—then deal with him.

A difficult person's behavior is not condoned or excused. As I said earlier, help is available to those seeking it. This chapter deals with how we can make a positive difference. We must not put ourselves in a position to be mistreated or exploited. With God's help, however, we can learn to see our difficult people through different eyes and turn our negative encounters into more positive ones.

8
Computers
and Tractors

WRITING IS THERAPY for me. Often when I find myself confused or in one of my melancholy moods, I'll break out my laptop computer and begin to hack away. For the past seventeen years I've been hacking away on something. Before my computer it was just a worn-out typewriter, but I still hacked. Hacking helps me crystallize what's inside my mind, and down through the years that's proven to be a most effective therapy. When my father needs to crystallize his thoughts, he heads up to his farm, hops on his John Deere tractor, and starts plowing a field; or he might fix some fence or work with the cattle he's raising. My dad says in his own eloquent way, "There's just something about being on a farm that helps a man to clear his mind."

If something ever happened to my laptop computer, it would be like losing a part of me; and if my dad were told tomorrow that he could no longer go back to his farm, I believe he would die sooner rather than later. In a way, my computer and my dad's farm have become intimate friends. And do you know why? Because they're good listeners. That's right. Good listeners. My dad and I are constantly drawn back to them because they will always allow us to be transparent without trying to control our response. They silently motivate us to divulge our thoughts and probe deep within ourselves for the solutions to our problems. Not once has my computer tried to dazzle me with all the right answers to my manifold questions; yet when I depart from it, I often have new insight. My dad's farm doesn't even talk back, but it has assisted him in making some of his life's toughest decisions. A good listener does much the same.

My friend Dr. Morris Alexander is a good listener. I've known Morris since college. He's always been a good listener. Now he is a professional listener—a clinical psychologist by trade. Over the years Morris has become a virtual unloading ground for me. He usually doesn't say much. He simply affirms, validates, and directs—which never requires excess commentary. On numerous occasions I have disclosed serious personal dilemmas to him. Not once has Morris given me pat answers. He does tune in to me, though, then asks strategic questions prompting me to probe deep inside myself for my own solutions. When conversing with Morris, I recognize that he is giving me his full attention, and I am assured he will keep my confidences—not an easy assignment. Because of this, I have returned to Morris again and again, and he has become one of my closest friends.

Everyone needs a Morris in his life. Everyone needs to be a Morris to somebody. It's risky. It takes personal security to be a deep listener. The rewards, however, are boundless. Good listeners have a record of rising to the top.

In researching his book *In Search of Excellence*, Tom Peters studied several of the world's top corporations for secrets to their success. One of his conclusions was that in the overwhelming majority of the cases, top executives were excellent listeners. The renowned Wilson Mizner once said, "A good listener is not only popular everywhere, but after a while he knows something." Good listeners become popular people, because others are attracted to them just like my dad and I are attracted to the farm and the computer. They also become smarter and more effective people. If this is true, then it behooves us to learn some basic listening skills.

FIVE CHARACTERISTICS OF GOOD LISTENERS

1. Understand now, reply later.
Good listeners do more than take in information. They seek to crawl into the skin of the speaker and reach a level of connectedness with him or her. Stephen Covey, an expert on listening, said:

> Seek first to understand and then to be understood. Most people do not listen with the intent to understand; they listen with the intent to reply. They're either speaking or preparing to speak. They're filtering ev-

erything through their own paradigms, reading their own autobiography into other people's lives.

I call this trespassing on others' thoughts. This is when the average listener tries to read into the other person his or her own experience and feelings instead of placing him- or herself in a position to fully understand where the speaker is coming from. One of the reasons we tend to have this problem is because when someone unloads on us, we feel a need to fix them. And the only way we can fix them is to draw from our own limited experiences. When we can't match experiences, we often feel disconnected from the speaker, as if we have nothing to offer. In most cases, however, the speaker doesn't want to be fixed but rather understood and empathized with. Offering quick, pat advice frequently makes listeners look shallow and unconcerned.

2. Control your negative emotions.

While it is important to demonstrate positive emotions such as compassion and empathy, it is equally important to control our negative emotions. Certain words, issues, or people can activate our negative emotions. When negative emotions are activated, we tune out, distort, or prejudge the message, which hinders us from making an accurate interpretation. I was involved in an incident recently that demonstrates this point clearly. An acquaintance of mine and I were engaged in a deep political conversation. It started off friendly but something I said pushed his negative emotional button and he went ballistic. His countenance literally changed in front of my face. He went from a person who respected my views to being totally intolerant. The reasoning, respecting, and listening was finished, and the conversation was over. If we had been able to listen to one another and respect each other's views, we could have agreed to disagree and still be friends. Possibly I could have been persuaded to move to his side of the political fence. Instead, his negative reaction drove me away.

To control our negative emotions, it is necessary to recognize what activates us and then develop personal boundaries and responses that protect us but at the same time allow us to listen more carefully and objectively.

. . .

3. Maintain confidentiality.

Becoming a good listener requires responsibility and self-control. This means always keeping the speaker's confidence. If it ever gets out that you broke a confidence, and it usually does, it will not be long before you will be labeled as untrustworthy. A surefire way to be a good confidant is to keep the fact that you are a confidant a secret.

4. Become a "whole-body" listener.

Good listening requires more than just using the ears. It requires all of us. Our ears, eyes, body, and mind must be tuned in. Good listeners give nonverbal as well as verbal clues that they are listening. Even when we are not saying a word, we are communicating how interested we are.

5. Fulfill the listening circle by responding and asking strategic questions.

A while back I met with a man to discuss a personal dilemma of mine. He had agreed to meet with me, so I trusted that he was interested in listening to me or he would have said he was busy. For the first several minutes of our meeting, I emptied out my soul to him. The whole time, however, he never really looked me in the eye. He was constantly glancing here and there, looking outside the window. Then, in the midst of my soul-wrenching disclosure, he started talking about something totally alien to what I was saying. Talk about a letdown! It was like someone had taken a needle and punctured my birthday balloon. He wasn't interested in me or my dilemma. Then I started feeling awkward and self-conscious, so I closed up. He continued to ramble and ramble and ramble. We never really discussed my dilemma, and I left thoroughly disappointed. What did he do? Or should I say: What didn't he do? He never fulfilled the listening circle by responding or asking questions. Nor did he let me finish speaking, and his body language was sending me a clear message: "I'm more interested in me and my problems than in helping you."

The ultimate characteristic of a good listener is the ability to prompt the speaker to look within him- or herself for answers. This comes about by completing the listening circle, asking strategic questions and showing whole-body language. Asking questions and maintaining proper body language does several things. It lets the speaker know that the listener is tuned in. It also helps the listener to focus more on what the speaker is saying. To complete the listening circle effectively, one cannot be a mere surface listener.

Good listening does not come easy, but the rewards far outweigh the sacrifices. Wilson Mizner's quote is worth repeating: "A good listener is not only popular everywhere, but after a while he knows something."

9
Appreciation
for Appreciation

WHEN THE MIRACLE happened, I was overjoyed. I couldn't believe it was actually true. I—Max Davis—finally had a university degree! To this day I don't know if it was an act of God or if the professors were just tired of seeing me. Anyway, as a demonstration of my joy, I dropped a note of gratitude to my favorite high school teacher, Mrs. Hammonds. If it wasn't for her, I wouldn't have made it to college, much less through it. During my senior year, she went the extra mile for me and helped me understand an extremely difficult subject—a subject I needed in order to be accepted into college. Mrs. Hammonds regularly met me before class. Several times during the semester, she took time out of her schedule to work with me after school. I reminded her of her sacrifices in my note.

A few days later, to my surprise, I received a letter of response back from her—a letter that forever affected my perspective on personal relations. She had since retired and wrote how much my note meant to her. She explained that in her thirty-something years as a teacher, she received very little gratitude. She told how she had given her life to teaching, only for most of her pupils to forget her. I'll never forget the last line of her letter. "Thanks for making one old, worn-out schoolteacher so happy." Read it one more time, but slowly. "Thanks for making one old, worn-out schoolteacher so happy." Could you hear the appreciation ringing in that statement? This woman really appreciated being appreciated. What a revelation!

Ever since then I've made it a point to try to show people gratitude for even the little things they do for me. Never, in my wildest dreams, though, could I have imagined the positive returns on what has seemed my small and insignificant efforts. It's amazing how far people will go when they know they are being appreciated. In his book *Loving Each Other*, Gary Smalley presents this interesting fact:

A survey was recently taken among several thousand workers, asking what their employers could do to motivate them to work harder. The employers were amazed that the number-one response had nothing to do with income or benefits. The majority of workers stated that the one thing their employers did to make them want to work harder was to express appreciation for their individual efforts.

Mary Kay Ash, founder of Mary Kay Cosmetics, built a multimillion-dollar corporation on this philosophy. Mrs. Ash states in her autobiography:

We've found that housewives who are getting into the job market for the first time thrive on the praise and appreciation we give them. No housewife ever has anyone in her family exclaim, "Oh, what a beautiful clean floor!" . . . The only time anybody ever notices housework is when you don't do it. Let's face it, housework is a thankless and endless job! Women need recognition for their achievements. I've seen women work harder for a ribbon than they would have for an expensive gift or a cash prize. We find that very often it isn't the money that motivates a woman but appreciation and recognition.

Think about it. If gratitude motivates people in the workplace—if million-dollar corporations are being built on it—imagine the effect gratitude can have on our personal relationships. It's a simple fact of life: People need to be appreciated. And when you give gratitude, people take note and they don't forget.

Being a person of gratitude, however, is not as easy as it may seem. For some it is downright difficult. Genuine gratitude is more than just saying "thank you" or "job well done." It is a way of life. It springs from within—from a deep appreciation of life and who you are as a person. This, in turn, flows over into other areas of our lives. If you are personally discontented with life, it is virtually impossible to give authentic gratitude to others. The more we begin to appreciate life, the easier it is to show gratitude to others.

Contrary to the materialistic society in which we live, there is a rich abundance of joy that is not spawned from fame or fortune but from simplicity—the scent of a rose, the laughter of a child, the freshness after a rain, or autumn leaves. Year after year we hear of millionaires and movie stars committing suicide, divorcing, entering drug rehabilitation, and so on. Why? It's because in all of their fame and fortune and abundance of "things," they could not find happiness. Guess what? It's not there. They missed the simplicity of real life.

A life of authentic gratitude begins with childlike simplicity. Christ said, ". . . unless you change and become like little children, you will never enter the kingdom of heaven" (Matthew 18:3). Now understand, volumes could be written on the kingdom of heaven. I will condense it down to one sentence. The kingdom of heaven is not just eternity with God after we die but joy, peace, and contentment right here on Earth. And to enter takes childlikeness. But what is childlikeness? Surely it is not irresponsibility. The apostle Paul wrote that as a man, he had no use for childish things. So the childlikeness Christ was talking about was different from the irresponsibility Paul was talking about. What was Christ talking about then? Here's what I believe.

All children I have ever known have had two absolute qualities. First, they have pure faith. They simply believe. They believe in God. They believe in Santa Claus. They believe in the tooth fairy and the Easter bunny. They believe in their parents. Unless some adult takes it from them, within every child is the supernatural ability to believe. Second, they are absolutely enchanted with life—not money, not career, not prestige—but simply life. They are fascinated with flowers and rocks and butterflies and the like.

My wife and I have three children, ages ten, seven, and four. We live in the country on seventy acres, and it seems like every other day they pick us a bouquet that's a mixture of flowers and weeds. They don't know the difference. They burst into the house with excitement on their faces, as if they have discovered a treasure chest of rare coins. Of course, we put the bou-

quet directly on the kitchen table for all to see.
These kids love life. They appreciate the simple.
As adults, the more our spiritual vision becomes
childlike, the more we will begin to see the mi-
raculous in the ordinary. This will produce a
deep sense of appreciation for life.

Growing in this capacity of gratitude will
propel us into richer relationships with others
and help us develop a natural appreciation for
God, ourselves, family, friends, nature, and hu-
mankind. As our natural gratitude grows in our
hearts, offering it to others will become a mere
formality.

10
Total
Freedom

To START THIS CHAPTER we're going to play a little game. I say a word and then I guess what comes to your mind first. Ready? First word. Exercise. Half of you thought "drudgery." The other half thought "healthy and feels great." Not bad, right? Okay. Second word. Church. Some of you thought "boring." Some of you thought "hypocrites." Others thought "God, Christianity, important." Hey, I'm pretty good at this. Third word. Discipline. Some of you thought "punishment." Some of you thought "training." A few of you thought "an educational discipline, like medicine or history." I guarantee, though, none of you thought "freedom." Yet freedom is what discipline is all about.

In the past, when I heard the word "discipline," scenes would flash across my mind of a drill sergeant yelling down a private's neck "Move it! Move it! Move it!" It wasn't until later on in life that I learned the power of discipline and how it can transform an ordinary life into an extraordinary one.

Actually, the word "discipline" is a combination of two words: *discipulus*, which means "student," and *discere*, which means "to learn." Webster defines discipline as "training that corrects, molds, perfects." So training, reproof, and learning are, in fact, all major elements of discipline. It doesn't sound like there's much excitement in discipline. Nevertheless, freedom is a direct by-product. When applied, discipline always brings freedom to the particular area exercised. There is no freedom without discipline. It seems like a contradiction, I know, but it's not.

When I was in undergraduate school, I had a real yearning to play the guitar. At that point in my life, having the gift of music would have been the ultimate. So I became a student, watching and trying to imitate every guitar player I saw. When my progress was slow, I became frustrated. Then one day I met a fellow student who became an inspiration. This guy could really play. He wasn't just good, he was genuinely great. He was a music major, and he taught guitar classes to help pay for his tuition. Every so often he did live concerts in the university theater, and it would be almost packed. Today he is a studio musician in Nashville. One day I said to him, "Man, you have such talent. It seems playing comes so easy to you." I'll never forget his response. I've reflected back on it time and time again. He said, "Max, it's one percent talent and ninety-nine percent discipline. I've practiced four to eight hours a day for over ten years. I enjoy it, but guitar playing is hard work." My friend's discipline brought him freedom in guitar playing. By sticking with his goal, day after day, year after year, his fingers slowly began to progress to where they eventually had total latitude on the guitar neck. Because of discipline, he was free to play virtually anything he wished.

The principle of discipline is important in all areas of our lives. Nothing worth accomplishing or having ever comes easy. Life just doesn't work that way. The sooner we realize this, the faster we will be on the road to success. A great marriage doesn't just happen. It takes work, planning, sacrifice, and commitment—in other words, discipline. An Olympic athlete didn't get to the Olympics by frolicking around.

I have another friend who is a novelist and recently had a series of books published by a prominent publishing house. He is bombarded almost daily by people who are "wannabe" writers. Most of these writers are big talkers, but very few are willing to pay the price for success. His story is strikingly similar to my guitar friend's story. It took my writer friend years and hundreds of rejection notices before he finally got published. But he hung in there, never gave up, and disciplined himself to write at least five pages a day. To this day, regardless of how uninspired he may feel, he forces himself to write five pages a day. In his own words, he says, "It's the discipline of writing those five pages a day that's important, not being inspired. Nine times out of ten the inspiration follows." Inspiration follows discipline. Now that's a gold nugget of wisdom! To a writer, inspiration is freedom because when one is inspired, writing ceases to be drudgery and begins actually to become fun. But usually it happens only after discipline has been applied to the situation. Discipline never seems fun at the time we are applying it. However, later on it produces fruit in our lives which makes our lives more satisfying.

Three central areas of our makeup require consistent discipline if we are to experience total freedom in our lives: mental/spiritual renewal, vocational discipline, and physical discipline.

MENTAL/SPIRITUAL RENEWAL

ROMANS 12:2 INSTRUCTS US, "Do not conform any longer to the pattern of this world, but be transformed by the renewing of your mind, then you will understand what the will of God is." In plain, practical language, something transcendental happens when we get alone with God and renew our minds. This principle of discipline has been used by successful people for centuries because it works. It's so easy to conform to the pattern of this world. It takes no

effort. The natural daily grind of the world system pulls and tugs and bids for us to submit to
its urgency. Also, the people in our life circle
have a way of crowding us, either consciously
or subconsciously, into the molds they have created for us. It takes deliberate effort to say no to
these external pressures and people and to find
"alone" time for ourselves and God. But it's
worth the effort. There's power in this discipline. Our inner self is renewed. Our creative
self is unleashed. We become transformed and
can then understand the will of God. This renewal process gives us the courage to continue
on a given path or to change course if necessary.
After we renew our minds we will know, by a
deep peace in our heart, what we are supposed
to do in certain areas of our lives. David
Schwartz, Ph.D., said in his book *The Magic of
Thinking Big:*

Take time out to confer with yourself
and tap your supreme thinking power.
Managed solitude pays off. Use it to re-
lease your creative power. Use it to find
solutions to personal and business problems. So spend time alone every day just

for thinking. Use the thinking technique all great leaders use. Confer with yourself.

I would like to take this powerful quote one step farther. Confer with yourself and with God. Renewing the mind involves meditation upon scripture, great literature, and silent reflection. It is there, in solitude, that our values are established, creative ideas are unleashed, goals are developed, and important decisions are made. This time alone is critical to a balanced, healthy life. Otherwise, we will be tossed back and forth by the pressures and demands of life, ever striving but never able to come to any real stability. God speaks when we are quiet—when we are still. Once I heard a song on the radio that really grabbed my attention. The chorus went something like this: "God loves to talk to little boys while they are fishing." The implication is that about the only time little boys are still enough for them to hear God is when they are fishing. So God takes advantage of that time. All of us would do better if we spent just a little more time being still and silent, maybe even more time fishing. Alexander Graham Bell, one of the greatest inventors of our time, said,

"Don't keep forever on the public road. Leave the beaten track occasionally and dive into the woods. You will be certain to find something that you've never seen before." I wonder how many inspirational ideas came to Mr. Bell's mind as he tromped through nature and meditated? Practically speaking, most of us can't just dive into the woods, but we can find a place of solitude. We have a choice: Conform to the system or be transformed.

VOCATIONAL DISCIPLINE

VOCATIONAL DISCIPLINE HAS to do with discovering your gifts and talents and then becoming an expert at them. It's paying the price for success. It is here, though, that we must be careful and use our common sense. In good faith we have been encouraged by parents, loved ones, and success promoters that we can do whatever we set our minds to do. But this is only a partial truth. In reality, we can't do whatever we set our minds to do. It would not be wise for a deaf person to aspire to be a commercial airline pilot. Unless a miracle happened, and hearing was restored, the person would be wasting his time. Safety rules and regulations require pilots to have accurate hearing. So it would be a waste of time and energy for that person to apply the principle of discipline in that area.

However, each one of us has unique abilities and gifts. When we can tap into that for which we are best suited and then apply the principle of discipline to that area, our potential then becomes unlimited. It is vital to explore our personality traits and abilities and make sure we are applying our energies in the proper direction. Applying the first discipline—mental/spiritual renewal—consistently will aid in helping us discover what it is we are truly meant to do with our lives.

In the book *Getting Rich Your Own Way,* Dr. Srully Blotnick compiled a study of 1,500 men and women who were observed for twenty years, from their early twenties to their early forties. Out of the 1,500, 83 became millionaires. Almost all of the millionaires surprisingly had one major attribute in common. None of them tried to get rich. What they did, however, was find out what they were good at and loved;

then they specialized in it. Because they loved what they were doing, over the years they became proficient at it. Naturally, money followed. This does not mean all of us who do what we are good at will get rich financially. For example, you may be gifted in the area of nursing, teaching, or carpentry. You might not become a millionaire doing these things, but by applying the discipline principle to what you are naturally inclined to, you will become proficient and make a respectable living producing vocational satisfaction.

It might be unrealistic to do what you are best suited for right away. The real world places real demands on us. We have bills to pay and obligations to meet. If this is the case, start doing what you love as a volunteer or a hobby. If you are persistent, it could turn into a real cash cow, eventually allowing you to do it full time.

Pete Babcock had the dream of someday being an NBA basketball head coach. But he had one thing going against him—he was just a high school junior varsity coach. However, while he coached high school, he volunteered to do scouting for an NBA scouting service. After years of volunteer scouting, doors slowly began to open. One thing led to another and eventually he was hired as an assistant coach for the San Diego Clippers. Now Pete is the vice president/general manager of the Atlanta Hawks. In the book *Storms of Perfection,* Pete said: "Looking back, I feel my patience and persistence through volunteer and part-time work helped me develop an attitude that you truly can find a way to 'live your dream.'"

Success follows those who work hard at what they are good at. But it requires two key steps:

1. Evaluate your abilities and loves and determine what it is you are really good at.
2. Apply the principle of long-term discipline to your abilities. Work hard. Become focused, as my writer and guitar friends did.

PHYSICAL DISCIPLINE

EXERCISE AND DIET is one of those areas we are usually not consistent in because we don't view it as critical. But our physical vitality directly impacts the other facets of our lives. The way we perceive our bodies—our endurance level—our energy level—all play a role in our effectiveness as a person. Chronic fatigue is one of the great killers of romance and vocational success. If we are not keen physically, we won't be keen mentally and emotionally. Numerous studies have concluded that consistent exercise and eating right is good for blood-sugar control, sexual performance, the immune and circulatory systems, reducing stress, losing weight, gaining muscle tone, and reversing depression.

Despite these facts and America's fascination with fitness, we are still dreadfully out of shape. The U.S. Department of Health and Human Services shows that over 85 percent of Americans do not get enough exercise, and more than a third of all Americans are obese. The big excuse is "I just don't have the time." However, by not taking the time to exercise and eat right, we lose down the road in the form of sickness, lack of energy, poor self-esteem. It's hard to feel good about ourselves when our body is sluggish and we don't feel our best.

Am I saying that we all have to look like

supermodels to feel good about ourselves? Certainly not. It is quite possible to be overweight and be a wonderful, successful, well-adjusted person. Some of the most delightful and successful people I know are overweight, but they have accepted their body and have developed a positive self-image. Yet, having said that, listen carefully to what Dr. Alan Loy McGinnis, one of the country's leading counselors, says in his book *Confidence:*

> People with good self-images tend to eat better and exercise more than those with low self-confidence. I am not a medical doctor, but I often ask depressed patients what they've eaten in the last 24 hours and about their exercise habits. The way they are taking care of themselves is one of the best tipoffs as to the state of their self-images.
>
> An astonishing number of us abuse our bodies with an almost self-destructive bent, and we eat so poorly and exercise so negligently that our bodies are giving us all sorts of sluggish sensations, headaches, pains, and general lassitude. We cannot

feel very positive about ourselves with all that going on.

In reality, exercise does not take that much time. Twenty to forty minutes of light-to-moderate cardiovascular activity five days each week, coupled with proper diet, will provide all the health benefits that the Olympic marathoner gets but with a much lower chance of injury or burnout. Dr. Kenneth Cooper, the father of modern-day aerobics, says walking three miles in forty-five minutes, five days a week, is all the aerobic conditioning anybody needs. Remember, consistency is the key.

One of the major fitness misconceptions is "More is better." Huge mistake! This probably leads to more injuries and negative attitudes toward fitness than any other single factor. More is *not* better, unless you are training for serious competition. We need to replace "more is better" with "consistency in conservative amounts goes a long way." This is true for cardiovascular aerobic work, weight and strength training, and, to a large extent, dieting. Don't be a shooting star—someone who tries to do too much too fast then burns out. It's better to discipline yourself to change your lifestyle gradually by being consistent. No matter what the intensity of the exercise, consistency is the key to success. The activity must be done three to five days each week for cardiovascular health and two to three days per week for strength.

Another key is to develop a long-term perspective. By having a long-term perspective, you can go easier on yourself. If you miss a day, don't get frustrated; just pick it up the next time around. This will add years and quality to your life.*

Applying discipline to these three areas—renewal, vocational, and physical—will transform your life. But it requires a lifestyle change—a change in priorities. You'll have to substitute one thing for another—maybe watch one hour of TV a day instead of two. Try it for a month. You'll never be the same! The key is to remember consistency and to give yourself a little bit

---

* Information on health/fitness gained with the help of Mike Kirtley, former Ironman Decathlon World Champion and currently head of one of the largest heart and fitness centers in the United States.

of grace from time to time. If you miss a day of renewal or exercise, don't sweat it; just pick up where you left off the next day. Soon you will find yourself more and more consistent.

Notes

11
KA-BOOM!

IT HAPPENS TO ME every so often, about once or twice a year. But this time, to be honest, it took me by surprise. It was as if a bomb suddenly dropped on a peaceful seaside resort. There I was just enjoying life, sipping tea by the sea, when all of a sudden ka-boom! A colossal bomb exploded. Sirens went off and there was a mad dash for shelter. My quiet afternoon in the sun had unexpectedly become a frantic race for survival.

That's the best way I can describe what happened. My life was going fine, everything in order—or so I supposed—and then ka-boom! I was exposed to a realm of my personality that I had no desire to see. And ouch! It wasn't a pretty sight! What made matters even harder to handle was the instrument used for pointing out my blind spot was another human being.

I went through all the stages. First, I denied I had a problem. Surely this person was misguided. Then, as the truth set in, I felt a sickening pain pierce deep in my gut. It hurt, really hurt. A serious pity party ensued. All kinds of stupid stuff ran through my mind. "You're a lousy excuse for a human. Nobody likes you. Move away. Yeah, that's the ticket—relocate." The only problem with relocation, though, is that I'll be wherever I move. But, as I shamefully shuffled into my room and crashed on the bed for a good pout, something began to happen. A small voice said, "Maybe they're right. If you deal with this area of your life now, you will grow into a more effective person. But if you live in denial, you'll continue in this self-defeating pattern and hurt yourself and those around you."

Blind spots? Self-defeating patterns? Hurt those around me? Deal with it? These are some heavy-duty ideas. It sounds serious. But my little shortcomings are not that serious; it's just my personality. Besides, I can't change who I am. Everyone has personality quirks. Nobody's perfect. Right?

Why is it we are masters in denying and minimizing the impact of our negative behaviors? Why are flaws in our character so hard for us to admit? Could it be that dealing with them forces us to face the truth about ourselves, and sometimes facing the truth is a painful experience.

In the human relations training aspect of psychology, there is something called the *Johari window.* This term can help clarify what I am saying. (See diagram on next page.) It shows a window with four panes. This window represents the real you, and each one of the four panes represents a different aspect of your personality.*

Pane 1 represents areas of your life that you know about, you're okay with, and you allow others to see.

Pane 2 represents areas of your life that you do not know about—blind spots. However, others may see them clearly.

Pane 3 represents areas of your life that you

---

* Raymond J. Corsini, ed., *Encyclopedia of Psychology,* 2nd ed. (New York: John Wiley & Sons, 1994), p. 182.

know about but you do not allow others to see. They are hidden. These are areas that, for various reasons, you do not want to deal with.

Pane 4 represents areas of your life that are hidden to self and others.

I. Known to Others	II. Unknown to Self
III. Known to Self Hidden to Others	IV. Unknown to Self and Others

Most of us live in pane 1 but occasionally are exposed to panes 2 and 3. When we are, we are forced to face issues that we have hidden and think are tucked safely away, or issues we have been blind to. Sometimes these hidden issues hinder us from being whole people and having effective relationships. When faced with these hidden issues, we have a choice: to deal with them and become stronger or to deny them and continue in our self-defeating pattern.

With blind spots usually another person is involved who causes us to see an area of our personality we didn't know existed. This experience can be both painful and traumatic. When I entered counseling after the breakup of my first marriage, I found out things about myself that I had never known. For example, in my past I had been happy-go-lucky, with a lot of friends, very successful and fun to be around, I thought. But when my ideas or plans became threatened, I would become controlling in order to get what I wanted. Yet I never knew this because it was unconscious. Because my ex-wife was unable to state her needs and stand up to me, I controlled her for years, never realizing that I was dragging her wherever I wanted to go in life. When the counselor pointed this out to me, I was shocked. I never considered myself controlling. I loved people. I was a nice guy. I wanted to help people. However, the more I honestly examined myself, the more I saw they were right. The question was "What was I going to do about it?" Was I going to deal with the issue or just continue on repeating the same self-defeating behavior and hurt someone else?

In Chapter 2 we discussed the dangers of blame shifting. In this chapter we deal with denial. The two are so similar that they are often confused. Yet upon closer examination, we can see that they are quite different. When a person is in denial, he or she recognizes a negative behavior and concludes that the behavior is not a problem, or simply refuses to admit to it at all. Blame shifting, on the other hand, is the transference of responsibility for the behavior to another party or circumstance.

DANGERS OF DENIAL

MOST OF US maintain some degree of personal security in our lives, because we have become masters at pushing disturbing thoughts about ourselves and our situations into our subconscious. Instead of dealing with issues as they arise, we just press on with life, suppressing any suspicion that something's not right. Denial for many of us has simply become a part of our everyday existence. The problem with this pattern is twofold.

First, as time passes and we persist in denial, our senses dull; and we become closed to any data that challenges what we want to believe. This is a dangerous place to live, because the only regulation we then have is ourselves. There is no room left for genuine growth, and we stagnate in our own narcissism.

Have you ever known someone, perhaps middle aged, whom people have given up on because they refuse to deal with any of their personality flaws? After we get frustrated with them, we usually say to ourselves "It's no use trying to reason with them. That's just the way they are. They are not changing." Have you ever wondered why they are like that? They have lived in denial for so long, refusing to deal with issues in their personality, that it is now beyond them to grasp change.

A perfect analogy of this is what I call *sandbagging.* Ideally, an emotionally healthy person has an open line of communication between self, others, and God. This line of communication is like a river flowing freely. Each time a character concern comes to the surface, it's like placing a sandbag in the river of communication. If the concern is dealt with immediately, the sandbag is removed by a relatively simple process, with minimal pain. However, if the concern is not dealt with but denied, the sandbag stays, creating a blockage. Soon another sandbag is added, and another, and another. After years of sandbags, the flow of open, honest communication is reduced to a mere trickle and sometimes, in severe cases, is completely cut off. Obviously, dealing with one sandbag at a time, as it arises, is much easier than having to deal with a whole lifetime of buildup.

Second, if not dealt with in a timely manner, eventually these issues will explode, forcing us to face them whether we want to or not. Unfortunately, at this stage, when the explosion occurs, the shrapnel usually wounds other people as well—often the people we love the most.

There are many reasons why we choose to live in denial. All of us, from time to time, do. We may not have the strength or the self-confidence to face up to a fault. Possibly, we worry too much about what others think, or we are simply afraid of what we may find out about ourselves. It's not easy seeing ourselves honestly. It demands courage and humility. Being exposed to a personal flaw, regardless of how small, can be an overwhelmingly painful experience, and pain is not something most of us enjoy. So our natural tendency is to dodge the bullet if possible.

Still, denial is serious, and not dealing with issues as they arise can cause us untold heartache and difficulty down the road. Most certainly, denial will keep us from reaching our full capacity as a person. The bottom line is: We must acknowledge that all of us are imperfect humans with faults. When we grasp this fact, we can then accept that there may be areas in our own lives that need modifying. It is important to give ourselves the grace to make mistakes as well as to give grace to others for being less than perfect. Peter McWilliams wrote in his book, *Life 101:*

> If we didn't play this game of denial with ourselves, we would make mistakes when we made them, admit them freely, and ask not, "Who's to blame?" or "How can I hide

this?" but "What's the lesson in here? How can I do this better?" The goal becomes excellence, not perfection.

Before we can deal effectively with blind spots in our character, first we must become aware of them. If we could see those areas ourselves, it wouldn't be a blind spot. Therefore, the process of becoming aware is initiated by those close around us, our friends and family. Do you place yourself in a position to be willing to talk about areas in your life that need help, or are you closed to this? Ask God to give you the courage to become the best you can be. Allow loved ones in your life to fulfill the role of a loving advisor.

12
$1 Makes
a Big
Difference

THERE I WAS in New York City about to meet with the vice-president of one of the largest publishing companies in the entire world, The Hearst Corporation, publishers of *The New York Times, Cosmopolitan, Good Housekeeping,* and numerous other popular magazines. It was a wonder that their vice-president even agreed to meet with me. Yet he not only met me, he took two hours out of his busy schedule to advise me on the next move we should make with our year-old publication, *Enhance Magazine*. At that point *Enhance* was a local complimentary magazine supported solely on advertising. Our first year was moderately successful, but we were at the point of having to make some major adjustments if we were going to be successful over the long haul.

To my surprise, the first recommendation Hearst's vice-president made was for *Enhance* to convert from a complimentary magazine to a priced magazine. He said, "You need to put a value on your magazine, because people will respect it more if they have to pay for it—even if it's just a dollar. If it is free," he added, "they have no investment in it, therefore they do not treat it with the same regard. Putting a price on something gives it more perceived value, and people take it more seriously."

After our meeting, I spoke with several national advertisers to find out what they viewed as important when considering advertising in a publication. Obviously, the first thing they wanted to know was the target audience. Who is actually reading the magazine? Second, 100% said the same thing as The Hearst Corporation. When a magazine has a price tag, people take it more seriously; therefore the response to the advertising within is greater. A free publication usually doesn't have as much perceived value, so the response to advertising is much lower.

It's called the *value principle*. It makes sense to me.

This value principle works not only in business marketing but in our personal lives as well. Gary Smalley, author of *Love Is a Decision* and numerous other books on relationships, helps us grasp this point even further. Smalley travels extensively throughout the world conducting marriage and family seminars that have transformed the lives of thousands. For one particular television special, he borrowed a friend's Stradivarius violin to use as an illustration. His friend had the violin flown in—complete with its own "security guard"! During the seminar, while teaching on value and honor, Mr. Smalley held up the violin for the audience to observe, without revealing its true nature. It was old and scratched up, with no strings, so it didn't look particularly impressive. As he held it up, he noticed that the audience's response was minimal. He says, ". . . my holding up the violin didn't produce even one 'ah-h-h-h' gasp in the entire crowd. After all, they could see with their own eyes that it was an old violin." Then he began to explain that this was not just any old violin that he was holding. He told how there were only a few of them left in the world, and it was valued at $65,000. He then showed the audience the tiny inscription that said "Stradivarius." He continued, "A spontaneous, collective, breath-catching 'ah-h-h-h' reflex rifled throughout the crowd. Just a few moments before, it was just an old violin, not worthy of any special honor, but by attaching that word 'Stradivarius' to it, it suddenly was given a high place of honor by everyone in the room."

YOU ARE A STRADIVARIUS

IN ORDER TO have effective relationships with others, it is imperative that we have a positive relationship with ourselves. This relationship begins by attaching high value to ourselves. We must stop seeing ourselves as old, beaten-up violins and start seeing ourselves as Stradivarii. I'm not talking about egotism or conceit or even pride, but a genuine sense of personal worth. People who possess a genuine sense of personal worth are secure. This security results in the ability to give of themselves to others. They are capable of love and attract healthy people. Because they are secure, they do not have to focus on themselves all the time. A person with low self-worth, however, often devalues others in an attempt to feel important. He or she also will spend vast amounts of time and energy trying to prove worthwhile by endeavors that will unquestionably leave him or her feeling empty and alone. The truth is that all of us, regardless of our accomplishments or backgrounds, are Stradivarii. The hard part is convincing ourselves of the fact.

WHERE DOES GENUINE SELF-WORTH ORIGINATE?

As I SAID EARLIER, I am not a doctor or psychologist. I'm simply an ex-pastor and businessman who has learned a whole lot from his mistakes. For years I've personally searched for self-worth. I've battled insecurity all my life. I still do. But over the years, the one and only place I've found total security and self-worth is in a relationship with the living God. My faith didn't come out of a blind leap either; I wanted facts. For probably ten years after I acknowledged my faith in God, I continued to search. With a skeptical but unbiased attitude, I researched miracles. I interviewed people who had experiences. I researched historical accounts and biblical accuracy. I even did an all-out scientific study in graduate school.

My findings were astounding and only confirmed my faith. When I began to consider the infinite order and complexity in the universe, it led me to one obvious conclusion: Some greater intelligence created life. The bottom line of my reasoning was: Throughout time, not even once has order ever come about from disorder. Wherever order exists, there is always some type of intelligence behind it.

Let me give you just a few examples. If you took fifty rocks, placed them in a bag, shook the bag up, and threw the rocks on the ground, how many times would you have to shake the rocks and drop them before they would land on the ground, by chance, spelling out your name in perfect order? A million times? A billion times? The fact is, it would *never* happen, because order doesn't come from disorder.

Now, suppose we wanted to build a house, and we put all the elements of the house in a huge box. In the box were nails, boards, shingles, wires, pipes, stoves, ovens, carpet—everything needed to construct a house. Next we attached the box to a helicopter and flew thirty feet in the air and dropped all the elements on the ground. What are the odds that the elements would fall together forming the house in complete functioning form? As with the previous example, it would never happen. Why? Because it takes intelligent life behind the elements to construct a house.

Creation of life is much more complex than a bag of rocks or a house. So, it stands to reason that intelligence is behind it as well. But hold on, I'm not the only one who thinks this. Some of the greatest minds in the world are in agreement with me. Here are just a few.

Thomas Jefferson said:

> When we take a view of the universe, in its parts, general or particular, it is impossible for the human mind not to perceive and feel a conviction of design, consummate skill, and indefinite power in every atom of its composition.

Astronomer Fred Hoyle notes the incredible way carbon manages to form and then just avoids complete conversion into oxygen:

If one atomic level had varied half a percent, life would have been impossible. . . . Some super-calculating intellect must have designed the properties of the carbon atom. . . . The carbon atom is a fix. . . . A common sense interpretation of the facts suggests that a super-intellect has monkeyed with the physics.

According to astronomer Pierre Simon de La Place:

The proof of an intelligent God as the author of creation stood as infinity to one against any other hypothesis for ultimate causation.

Stephen Hawking, a British physicist called the Einstein of our day, has said:

The odds against a universe like ours coming out of something like a Big Bang are enormous. I think there are clearly religious implications.

The physicist P. C. W. Davies wrote of the universe's physical processes:

> How they are fine tuned to such stunning accuracy is surely one of the great mysteries . . . had this exceedingly delicate tuning of values been slightly upset, the subsequent structure of the universe would have been totally different. Extraordinary physical coincidences and apparently accidental cooperation offer compelling evidence that something is going on. . . . A hidden principle seems to be at work.

The Bible says it this way: "For since the creation of the world God's invisible qualities—his eternal power and divine nature—have been clearly seen, being understood from what has been made" (Romans 1:20).

If you are still not convinced, here are a few more facts on the creation of man.

According to the Brain Research Institute of the University of California at Berkeley, the potential of the human brain to create, store, and learn may be virtually unlimited. The prominent scholar Ivan Yefremov, of the former Soviet Union, has said, "Throughout our lives we use only a fraction of our thinking ability. We could, without any difficulty whatever, learn forty languages, memorize a set of encyclopedias from A to Z, and complete the required courses of dozens of colleges."

The average brain only weighs about three pounds, but it contains over 12 billion cells. Each cell is connected to over 1 billion other cells, totaling 120 trillion brain connections. One scientist said, "The human brain is the most complex arrangement of matter in the universe." Dr. Gehard Dirks, who holds fifty IBM computer patents, said studying the functions of the human brain gave him most of his ideas for inventions. Commenting on the brain's complexity, he stated, "If we could invent a computer that would duplicate the capabilities of the human brain, it would take a structure the size of the Empire State Building just to house it."

No one can convince me that the complexity of the human brain, with all its emotional and reasoning abilities, is a mere accident.

All the greatest scientific minds combined

could never build a human brain. The best they could do is build a supercomputer, yet they would still have to program it with human intelligence. But who programmed us? Where did our intelligence come from?

I would have to write another book if I were to give details on our circulatory system, the eye, the ear, the reproductive system, our cellular structure, or our plumbing. Nor can I write of the numerous improbable life-supporting complexities of good ol' mother earth. The truth is, life in every form, from the single cell to the human brain, is a fabulous miracle.

I've said all this to convince you that each and every one of us is most definitely a Stradivarius. Think about it. We are complex. We are marvelous. We are fearfully and wonderfully made! The God of the universe created us, and that fact alone gives us self-worth. Social psychologist David G. Myers has determined that self-worth boils down to a simple, but unlikely, statement of good news, which he presents in his book *The Pursuit of Happiness:*

The universe has a Creator whose extraordinary love compelled this Spirit-

Being to assume a human form, to experience suffering, and to break the bonds of death, thereby assuring us that we matter, that we are accepted, that we can live with hope. The radical and liberating implication: No longer is there a need to define our self-worth solely by our achievements, material well-being, or social approval. To find self-acceptance we needn't be or do anything. We need simply to accept that we are, ultimately and unconditionally, accepted.

The story of Pinocchio is a great example of our need for acceptance. As Pinocchio ponders his life, he flounders in a terrible confusion about his self-worth. Finally he turns to his maker, Geppetto, and reflects, "Papa, I am not sure who I am. But if I'm all right with you, then I guess I'm all right with me."

Let the value principle work for you. As you discover and live with a healthy self-worth, then you can begin to see the same value in those around you.

13
Four
Damaged
Vehicles

OURS IS A SOCIETY of momentary whims, quick trips to the Fast Stop, thirty-second bank transactions, and McDonald's. We're a people on wheels and we're movin'! Unfortunately, in this hurry-up world of ours, it seems that patience is an almost-forgotten virtue. We get irritated if we have to wait in line for more than three minutes at the local fast-food chain; look out if we get stuck behind some poor old lady while driving in traffic. It's ridiculous, the pace at which some of us are moving through life. And all too often this fast-paced living has taken its toll. It not only strains us physically and emotionally, but it strains our relationships as well.

Patience, or impatience, is something I've personally been dealing with for quite a while — actually, my whole life. It's tough. Just when I think I've got it, I lose it again. Once, being in such a hurry to get home, I began weaving in and out of traffic trying to make some time, when I rear-ended a police car. He in turn rear-ended a pickup truck, which rear-ended another police car. A total of four vehicles were involved, including two police cars! Later, when contemplating why I was in such a rush to get home, I could not come up with any good reason, except that my whole life was one big rush, and it was killing me. I was becoming more and more impatient with my wife, my kids, and others. Yet my external impatience was a mere symptom of a much deeper problem. I was impatient with myself.

Too many of us are living that same routine. We think that by driving ourselves harder, we are getting ahead. In reality, we are only hurting ourselves and cutting our productivity. Most of us believe that if we slow down, things won't get done. This is not true.

For several years, I worked for the United Parcel Service, one of the country's leading delivery companies. The success of UPS is built on one central theme: punctuality. If UPS guarantees a delivery by a certain day, you can bank on it or your money back. Companies all across our land depend on UPS for their livelihood. It is a pressure-cooker job filled with more than its share of stress but also with financial rewards.

Drivers are pushed to the limit to perform at their optimal level, and only a few actually make it. However, UPS does not push its drivers in the traditional ways that other companies do. Their nontraditional approach is one reason why UPS has been a leader in the delivery business for decades. UPS has developed what it calls safe and effective work methods. Each delivery route is scientifically calculated down to the exact minute. Computers analyze precisely how many boxes, deliveries, and miles a truck needs to handle in a given amount of hours. In the morning, when drivers go in to work, a printout tells them exactly how many hours of work there are on the truck. If a driver has nine hours of work on a truck, she should be finished in nine hours. This is a great system. However, it hinges on one thing: the driver's ability to execute the work method effectively. The whole computer calculation is based on this concept.

The UPS work method is a system in which

drivers are taught to enter their truck in a specific way, record data in a specific way, pick up boxes in a specific way, put them down in a specific way, even walk at a certain pace. If drivers follow these work methods properly, then there is no need to speed, rush, or run. The key to the work method is patience. Most times when drivers push themselves too fast, they break the method and actually lose time, in addition to risking injury or an accident. At UPS, drivers are told time and time again, "Don't run or speed, just remember to be patient and apply the methods."

When I first went to work for UPS, I was fresh out of a college football career and was a pretty good athlete. "Surely the job would be a cinch for me," I thought. So at first I didn't take the methods too seriously. When I got to work each morning, I was ready to kick it as fast as I could. In my mind, I was going to break all kinds of delivery records. A funny thing happened, though. The more I killed myself trying to get ahead, the further behind I would get. Here I was a collegiate athlete, and most of the other drivers were doing better than I. For weeks I was frustrated. Then some of the more experienced drivers told me, more than once,

"Max, you have to stop trying to be super-driver; slow down, be patient, and do the work methods. Otherwise, you're going to burn out." Everyone knew I was working hard, but I wasn't working smart. When I finally decided to slow down and focus my energy on the methods, instead of trying to be super-driver, my times consistently dropped. I was even able to relax, enjoy my job more, and still finish ahead of schedule. It had nothing to do with racing through the day but rather with being patient and pacing myself.

Life works the same way. When we are driven by impatience, we tend to get stressed out and burned out; we injure ourselves, have accidents, and, most important, run over other people. The cost of impatience is high. Brian Adams, author of *The Illustrated History of the World* and many children's books, said, "Impatience breeds anxiety, fear, discouragement, and failure. Patience creates confidence, decisiveness and a rational outlook, which eventually leads to success." To maximize our personal growth, it is vital to understand the role that patience plays.

. . .

None of us is born instinctively patient. In fact, we are born just the opposite. I challenge you to show me an infant who, when hungry, will wait patiently without throwing a fit. You can't. When an infant is hungry, it wants its food now. An infant is playing a game of survival. It reacts instinctively. The only way to get its needs met is to demand. However, this approach only works for a short while. As time passes, the infant becomes more mature and realizes that life works through a structured system. He can't just go in his pants anymore. He has to use the toilet. He has to eat at the table at certain times and go to bed at certain times. A pattern of life begins to develop. Training takes place. Patience is learned in small ways. "You can have a cookie after you finish dinner," Mom says, or "We'll get that toy the next time we are at the store."

As our personality develops, many of us are inclined in one of two directions. We are either the strong-willed, high-energy type, who usually drifts toward impatience, or the compliant, passive type, who often takes on a more leisurely role. Taken to the extreme, both types are equally dangerous. Impatient types, like me, tend to want to get things done yesterday; passive types tend to say, "If we don't get it done today, we'll do it tomorrow or next week." Impatience is at one end of the stick, and passivity is at the other end. Our goal should be to fall somewhere in the middle, living as a balanced, patient person.

UPS required balanced patience—working with a sense of urgency yet applying self-control within the methods. The impatient person has no problem with the sense of urgency. It's the self-control that's the problem. The passive person handles the self-control but has a difficult time maintaining a sense of urgency. Balanced patience, however, is a blend of the two, an active state of realizing what needs to be done while applying wisdom and self-control to the implementation.

FOUR ELEMENTS OF BALANCED PATIENCE

BALANCED PATIENCE CONSISTS of four elements: time, vision, flexibility, and perseverance.

The Time Factor

Attaining anything worthwhile in life requires time. Whether it is losing weight, building a business, or seeing a relationship restored, the time factor must be considered. Because we live in an instant society, we have come to expect instant results. But rarely does anything of value come to us instantly; most worthwhile things take time.

A friend of mine pastors a 1,000-member church. I can remember when the church was struggling with fewer than thirty people. The pastor came to Tulsa with a vision for the city, a plan, a whole lot of patience; and he began to implement his ideas. For many years he and his wife held part-time jobs in addition to pastoring. After nearly twenty years of cultivating, which took a lot of sweat and sacrifice, their church has 1,000 members. It took time. I'm sure there were many days he was tempted to quit, but my pastor friend realized that if he was consistent and patient, eventually he would see his goals met.

My father-in-law loves cultivating trees and plants. We share seventy acres of land with him, and he always has some project going that involves planting. The other day we were talking about our vision for the property, and he was saying how it takes a lot of planning and patience to develop a beautiful piece of land. "The reason so many young people today don't have beautiful yards," he said, "is because they want it done right now without putting the time and effort into it. It takes a vision." Our instant society has even infiltrated our yard work. But my father-in-law has balanced patience and a vision for the next generation. He doesn't try to accomplish everything at once. Instead, he's steady and consistent, realizing he will be planting until he dies.

Developing healthy personal relationships also requires time and cultivation. When a couple experiencing marital difficulties goes into counseling, they often have the illusion that somehow the counseling is going to cure all their problems. After the counselor explains that it's going to take months of work and commitment on their part, many simply quit. But of those who decide to persevere through the program, many find rekindled love, and their relationship is stronger than before. The lost feelings don't just come back; they have to be cultivated and groomed. This requires work from both parties, time, and patience.

The same holds true for love maintenance. Love at first sight is highly overrated. Deep, abiding love is something that takes a lifetime to build. Each time a couple overcomes an obstacle or experiences a victory, love is solidified a little more. Anything worthwhile in life requires time to build. Understanding this principle helps us have patience. Because we don't expect instant results, we naturally slow down.

Vision

There is a difference between a lofty dreamer and a person who has a vision. A vision is a blueprint of where we want to end up. It's more than a goal. A vision or plan involves goals and also specific practical steps to achieving those goals. A vision for life comes about by knowing who you are and the areas in which you are gifted. It is vital that our vision lines up with God's design for us. When we impulsively jump from one plan to another, we waste our time. We can know what is best for us through mental/spiritual renewal, wise counsel, and self-evaluation.

Proverbs 29:18 says, "Where there is no vision, the people perish." Many people lack a vision for their lives. As a result, they don't have solid direction in life. It often has been said that average people spend more time planning a vacation than they do planning their lives. What a tragedy. What do you envision for your marriage and family? For your career? For your health? For your yard? We need a vision for every area of our life that we deem valuable. Without a vision, we perish. Why is having a detailed vision so important? A vision gives us organization, guidance, and energy—which has a calming effect on our lives. This helps us become more patient people.

Tom Morris said in his book *True Success, A New Philosophy of Excellence:*

> For a lot of people, life is a treadmill. No matter how fast they go, they get nowhere. And they feel they're getting nowhere. Every day is a whirlwind of activity, and yet the only discernible results of the frantic pace are exhaustion, confusion, frustration, and pain. But there is an alternative. As Mary Wollstonecraft Shelley pointed out

more than a hundred years ago: "Nothing contributes so much to tranquilize the mind as a steady purpose—a point on which the soul may fix its intellectual eye." The power of an inner vision is healing, tranquillity, new life, efficient direction, and real accomplishment. Off the treadmill and onto the path of true success.

Because a vision is detailed, it works much like the UPS work methods. When we have direction, we no longer have to race through life. Yes, we need a sense of urgency, but by understanding that the fulfillment of our vision requires time, we can apply self-control and pace ourselves and not experience burnout.

Matt weighed over 350 pounds, and it was killing him. He was dying both physically and emotionally. He tried numerous crash diets but always gained the weight he lost right back. Each time he regained weight, however, he would gain a little bit more than he originally lost. Finally he ended up in the hospital. His doctor told him that the key to losing weight and keeping it off was not crash diets but a day-to-day lifestyle change. The doctor explained,

"If it took you twenty-five years to put the weight on, what makes you think you can lose it in three months without doing serious damage?"

Matt realized his present state was not God's best, so he got a vision to lose one-half of his body weight. His doctor helped him set up a detailed program by which he would eventually fulfill his vision by reaching a series of small goals. Because Matt knew where he was going, he could pace himself so he wouldn't experience burnout. With the help of God and his doctor, Matt reached his goal eighteen months later. Now Matt doesn't worry about gaining the weight back because his whole lifestyle has changed.

Flexibility

Plan some obstacles into your visions. Realize that things happen out of your control. Don't be discouraged or deterred from your purpose by daily roadblocks. In the computer analysis that UPS uses to determine a truck's workload, it always plans a certain amount of time for unexpected delays. Traffic, the area of town, and stalls are all figured in.

Robert Schuller wrote in his book *Power Thoughts:* "Today remind yourself to expect setbacks. There will be obstacles in your way. There will be problems you have to solve. Expect them. Plan to stall. That's a sign of good management and wise leadership. No one goes from Point A to Point B without adjusting his course a little bit."

Having this mindset helps keep us on course. Temporary setbacks don't destroy our confidence because we know they are coming.

Perseverance
After reviewing the first three elements of balanced patience, it's obvious that an underlying factor in all three is perseverance. There is no such thing as patience without perseverance. The two go hand in hand. *Webster's* defines perseverance as: continuing forward in spite of difficulties. People who have perseverance win because they never give up. They may have to be flexible, make adjustments, and reroute some things, but they never give up.

Balanced patience will work in every area of life, from personal relationships to building a career. Let it change you. Remember:

- Anything worthwhile in life takes time.
- A vision will give your life structure, purpose, and direction.
- Pace yourself—with a vision there is no need to race through life.
- Be flexible—plan for setbacks and the unexpected.
- Persevere, persevere, persevere.

14
Failing
Forward

FAILURE. WHY DOES that word disturb us so much? Why are our lives so often driven by the fear of it? Could it be because we live in a "Just Do It!" age? Everywhere we turn, everywhere we look, we are bombarded by success promoters who tell us, "Reach for the stars! There's no limit to what you can accomplish if you only set your mind to it, and, of course, follow the right steps." We're encouraged to dream the impossible dream, think positive, talk positive, and substitute positive assertions about ourselves for negative inner dialogue. We are led to believe that to be happy and at peace, our ambitions must be realized, our children raised wonderfully, our marriage perfect, and our bank accounts fat. Many more of us fear failure because we feel we have to prove to ourselves and others that we are okay.

No doubt, there is a certain amount of wisdom in positive thinking. Enthusiasm, faith, and self-confidence all play an important role in balanced, healthy living. Critical, fatalistic doom and gloomers are a drain on themselves and others. So, with good reason, I urge you to try positive thinking, but with this stern warning: No matter how hard we try and how much we plan, no matter how many success tapes we listen to, no matter how positive our confession is, our lives will have their share of failures. There's no way around it. Things will not always turn out the way we planned. In fact, they probably *won't* turn out exactly the way we planned. Am I being pessimistic? Not at all. Understanding failure and how to deal with it is essential to authentic success. The way we handle failure and disappointment reveals our true character and profoundly affects the direction of our future.

To succeed in life, whether in our relationships or our careers, it is imperative that we allow ourselves and others a certain amount of room for failure, and then respond to it properly. Author and motivational speaker Richard J. Needham says, "Strong people make as many and as ghastly mistakes as weak people. The difference is that strong people admit them, and learn from them. That is how they become strong."

Johnson & Johnson, the world's largest and most successful health care company, has mastered this principle. In the March '95 issue of *Fortune Magazine*, J&J reported that its most valued assets were managers who had failed in a big way but had learned from their mistakes. The company views the cost of failure as tuition paid in the school of hard knocks. According to the article, after failure, managers usually become wiser and more proficient, so letting them go would be a big mistake.

Prominent talk show host Sally Jessy Raphael was told by professionals in the broadcasting business that she should "get a job as a secretary or a receptionist; they weren't using her style of women." She says, "That's when I first became acquainted with the 'R' word: Rejection." Over her long climb to the top she was fired eighteen times. Each time she was fired, however, she learned and became more determined than ever until she eventually reached her goal.

Volumes could be written on the vast number of men and women who have endured devastating failure but have risen from the ashes of despair to become great successes. Consider Abraham Lincoln, who failed constantly throughout his political career until he finally gave the presidency a go, or Thomas Edison, who when asked how it felt to fail over 1,000 times while inventing the lightbulb, replied, "The lightbulb was an invention of over 1,000 steps." Henry Ford failed so many times people thought he was a lunatic. All of these people shared one common ingredient. They learned to fail forward. The late Norman Vincent Peale coined the term. According to him, failing forward is learning from failure and using it creatively in the direction of eventual success.

Some of us have failed in friendships. Some of us have failed in marriage. Some of us have failed in business. Still others feel they have failed as parents. One thing is sure, though; all of us have, at one time or another, failed. Often after experiencing failure, the pain is so great we are tempted to wallow in our own self-pity and never get back on our feet to try to accomplish anything worthwhile again. Few of us realize the benefits of failure. Instead, we try to shield ourselves from it. But by learning to fail forward, we can turn our failures into stepping-stones to a much richer life.

WHAT FAILURE DOES FOR US

Failure directs us.
For some people, failure reveals the need to make adjustments. The vision we have is valid; but in order to reach our ultimate destination, a change in course is required.

Each fall for sixteen consecutive seasons, I played the game of football. God graced me with the ability to run. I was considerably faster than anyone in our school and was awarded a full scholarship to the University of Mississippi. My college coaches had a vision for me, and the school invested a lot of money in my abilities. Because I was fast, I was tried at many offensive positions, particularly running back. My problem was that I was small for a college player and had a hard time holding on to the football. When the force of guys weighing anywhere from 200 to 280 pounds jolted my 175 pounds, the impact often sent the ball flying. In high school I was highly recognized in the running-back position. In college, I was a failure at running back. Did this mean football wasn't for me, and the coaches made a mistake in recruiting me? Not at all. They experimented with me for a while and eventually assigned me to the defensive corner-back position. (For some of you reading who are not up on your football positions, that's the man who guards against the pass.) My speed was utilized and size was not a factor. Failure simply meant that some adjustments needed to be made in order to assure future success.

On the other hand, consistent failure could be sending us a clear message that we are heading down the wrong road completely and need to get off and find a new direction in life. Mark Twain once said, "If at first you don't succeed, try, try again. And then give up. There's no sense being a damn fool about it." This sounds pretty crude, particularly in our society, but accepting failure actually can be freeing if we allow it to be.

Consider the story of Theo. Steven Carter and Julia Sokol wrote about Theo in their book *Lives Without Balance:*

For ten years I tried to get established in the restaurant business. This may not seem like a big deal to some people, but to me, it was everything. My restaurant was my life.

And no matter what I did, I couldn't make it do any more than break even. I changed menus, changed staff, reorganized the kitchen. I advertised in print, on the radio. Everything. I was determined. But it didn't work. Finally I threw in the towel. Although I didn't know it at the time, it was the best day of my life.

For Theo, losing his dream was a liberating experience. It made him acknowledge that his dream had taken over his life. It had become this enormous brick wall against which he threw himself at regular intervals, only to get bruised again and again. Finally he walked away, and when he did, his life changed.

Theo is now working a regular job with regular hours and saving money instead of spending everything on his restaurant. His stress level is way down, and he is much happier. Theo says, "Everything is so much better now, and I'm so glad that I finally had the brains to walk away from it."

In our personal relationships, periodic failures usually are indicators that adjustments need to be made in our personalities in order to assure future success. Continued failure, however, may be an indication that we are in an unhealthy relationship and won't experience freedom until we become a whole person. For some, this means staying and working toward healing. For others, it may mean getting out of the unhealthy situation completely. Before making a life-changing decision, though, it is advisable to seek counsel from a professional who respects your personal convictions.

Failure motivates us.
As was stated earlier, Sally Jessy Raphael was fired eighteen times. Each time she was fired, however, she became that much more determined to make it. If we have a deep abiding

assurance that we are on the right path, that our goals are realistic and accurate, then failure can be a fantastic motivator for success.

Failure teaches us.
Failure gives us the opportunity to learn, and knowledge is power. Typically we learn much more from failure than we do from success. Obviously, success is more desirable than failure. But lasting success will likely have risen out of numerous failures along the way. Each time we fail, we learn a little more. So it makes sense that failure is a necessary ingredient for learning, which leads ultimately to success. For years the scientific community has affirmed this principle.

Dr. Keith Reemstma, chief of surgery at Columbia Presbyterian Hospital, has been working on a cure for diabetes for years. He hasn't found a cure yet, but he keeps on going, day after day, year after year. How does he do it? "I never think of what I do as failure," he says. "It's just an incomplete result. I always have in mind what I am trying to accomplish, and each experiment tells me a little bit more about what I have done wrong."

But how does this principle apply to our relationships? Obviously, we can't continue to fail over and over again with different people. It would be unethical to view people as object lessons for our ultimate success in relationships. Failure on a personal relationship level starts relatively small. If we deal with our mistakes as they happen and learn from them—instead of denying them—we assure growth for ourselves and our partner. Does all this sound familiar? It all gets back to the bottom line of identifying our self-defeating behaviors and dealing with them.

Failure humbles us.
Failure does a great job of stripping away the facades we sometimes hide behind. It deflates our arrogance and ego, which often is what we need to be more effective. After experiencing failure, we tend to listen more and are more empathetic to the needs of others. Failure reminds us that we, too, are human.

Since experiencing my broken years—spoken of in Chapter 1—I cannot begin to tell you how many hurting people have come across my path whom I have been able to encourage. Before my broken years, I was insensitive to the hurt that many people were going through. Enhance Publishing, which has a vision to reach hurting people with a practical message, came about as a direct result of my broken years. Failure broke me, but it also healed me.

When a fine stallion is broken by its master, none of its strength and beauty is impaired. It is simply brought under control and becomes useful for its appropriate purpose. A wild stallion has beauty and power as it runs unharnessed over the land. However, after it is broken, it becomes not only an object of beauty but a powerful instrument of use. If we humble ourselves and learn from our failures, no matter how devastating they may be, we will soon find ourselves like a fine trained stallion. We will have harnessed power from the knowledge gained through our experience, yet our humility will cause others to be attracted to us. Handling failure correctly will lead us to success and helps make us beautiful people.

It is critical to grasp what failure is and what failure is not. Success and failure are not antonyms. They work together hand in hand.

15

A Serious
Subject

As you can tell from my writing style, I like to add a dose of humor to some genuinely serious subjects. Humor often makes examination of ourselves more tolerable. In this chapter I tried to do that. I contemplated. I probed. I toiled. All to no avail. I could not do it. The subject is just too critical. It's the foundation of what this whole book is about. Without it you can toss the book in the trash because it won't work. So I'll keep this chapter short and to the point. The subject is humility.

Confucius wrote in 500 B.C., "Humility is the foundation of all virtues." John Buchan, British diplomat and author, declared, "Without humility there can be no humanity." Solomon taught that wisdom comes from humility and humility comes before honor. Christ said, "For he whoever exalts himself will be humbled, but whoever humbles himself will be exalted" (Matthew 23:12). As you can see, humility is a subject that great thinkers of our past took seriously.

In our quest for personal growth, humility must be at the foundation—for it is the core of moral character. Before proficiency is achieved, we must first admit to inadequacy. The more humble we become, the more quickly we will experience personal excellence.

FOUR QUICK POINTS OF HUMILITY

Humble people recognize their dependency on God. Dependency on God does not mean we shouldn't use our head. Our responsibility is to use the faculties that God gave us. Dependency is looking to God for direction and recognizing His ability to orchestrate the affairs of our lives—acknowledging God's role by seeking Him for direction instead of forging out on our own, creating our own destinies. When we acknowledge God in all our ways, He will direct our path and support us.

Humble people are secure in who they are.
Humble people do not belittle themselves. They do not act insignificantly or inadequately because they know they are valuable just as they are. Therefore, there is no need to prove anything or elevate themselves. They are secure.

Humble people are interdependent.
They are aware that they do not know all the answers and that there may be others who are more intelligent, have more experience, and are more gifted. They are not independent or codependent; they are interdependent. They are team players who perceive the value of input from others. Robert Schuller, the author of many books of inspiration, said, "Nothing is impossible—if I am humble enough and smart enough to get the right people to help me." In personal relationships, humble people understand the partnership ethic and do all they can to encourage their partner, yet they still take

care of themselves so they can be more effective.

Humble people are real.
Humble people have looked in the mirror of their souls, have taken an honest inventory of themselves, and realize they will always be working on themselves. They are *farmers* (talked about in Chapter 1). Keith Miller wrote in *A Hunger for Healing,* "Humility is seeing ourselves as we actually are, good and bad, strong and weak, and acting authentically on those truths."

Humble people are confident, yet they seek to serve others as well as themselves. They are aware that fulfillment is directly related to building up and encouraging others. Because of this attitude, others are naturally drawn to humble people. Humility is the first step toward growth. It is admitting that personal excellence is impossible without the power of God and the input of other people in our lives. If you want to experience life's best, develop the virtue of humility.

• • •